MONADOLOGY AND SOCIOLOGY

TRANSMISSION

Transmission denotes the transfer of information, objects or forces from one place to another, from one person to another. Transmission implies urgency, even emergency: a line humming, an alarm sounding, a messenger bearing news. Through Transmission interventions are supported, and opinions overturned. Transmission republishes classic works in philosophy, as it publishes works that re-examine classical philosophical thought. Transmission is the name for what takes place.

MONADOLOGY AND SOCIOLOGY

Gabriel Tarde
edited & translated by Theo Lorenc

re.press Melbourne 2012

re.press

PO Box 40, Prahran, 3181, Melbourne, Australia
http://www.re-press.org
© re.press 2012
The moral rights of the authors have been asserted

This work is 'Open Access', published under a creative commons license which means that you are free to copy, distribute, display, and perform the work as long as you clearly attribute the work to the authors, that you do not use this work for any commercial gain in any form whatsoever and that you in no way alter, transform or build on the work outside of its use in normal academic scholarship without express permission of the author (or their executors) *and* the publisher of this volume. For any reuse or distribution, you must make clear to others the license terms of this work. For more information see the details of the creative commons licence at this website:
http://creativecommons.org/licenses/by-nc-sa/3.0/

British Library Cataloguing-in-Publication Data
A catalogue record for this book is available from the British Library

National Library of Australia Cataloguing-in-Publication Data

Author: Tarde, Gabriel de, 1843-1904.

Title: Monadology and sociology / Gabriel Tarde ; translated by Theo Lorenc with afterword and notes.

ISBN: 9780980819724 (pbk.)
ISBN: 9780980819731 (ebook : pdf)

Series: Transmission.

Subjects: Sociology--Philosophy.
Monadology.

Other Authors/Contributors:
Lorenc, Theo.

Dewey Number: 301.01

Designed and Typeset by A&R

This book is produced sustainably using plantation timber, and printed in the destination market reducing wastage and excess transport.

CONTENTS

Translator's Preface   1

Monadology and Sociology   5

Afterword: Tarde's Pansocial Ontology   73

TRANSLATOR'S PREFACE

The text used for this translation is the 1895 edition of *Monadologie et Sociologie*, in Gabriel Tarde (1895) *Essais et mélanges sociologiques*, Lyon, A. Storck / Paris, G. Masson, pp. 309-389. This text is a reworked and expanded version of an article published in 1893 as 'Monads and Social Science' ('Les Monades et la Science Sociale'), *Revue Internationale de Sociologie*, vol. 1, no. 2, pp. 157-173 and vol. 1, no. 3, pp. 231-246. The earlier version corresponds to chapters I, IV, V and VI of the 1895 text. A small amount of material is in the earlier version of the text but not the later version; this is given in the notes to this translation (minor stylistic variants between the two are not noted).

Two modern editions of the original text are available: Éric Alliez (ed.), Le Plessis, Institut Synthélabo, 1999; M. Bergeron (ed.), Québec, Cégep, 2002, available at http://classiques.uqac.ca/classiques/tarde_gabriel/monadologie/monadologie.html).

These editions give no sources of Tarde's citations; J. Sarnes and M. Schillmeier's German translation (Gabriel Tarde, *Monadologie und Soziologie*, Frankfurt, Suhrkamp, 2009) gives a few but not all. I have attempted to trace all the citations, without complete success; however, it is likely that some passages marked as citations in the text are paraphrases rather than verbatim quotes. References given are to English translations where available.

Tarde uses the masculine gender throughout when referring to persons in general; the translation conforms to this usage.

I would like to thank Isaac Marrero-Guillamón and Dan Cryan for their assistance.

MONADOLOGY AND SOCIOLOGY

MONADOLOGY AND SOCIOLOGY

Hypotheses fingo[1]

I

The monads, children of Leibniz, have come a long way since their birth. By several independent paths, unremarked by scientists themselves, they slip into the heart of contemporary science. It is a remarkable fact that all the secondary hypotheses implicit in this great hypothesis, at least in its essentials if not in its strictly Lebnizian form, are now being proved scientifically. The hypothesis implies both the reduction of two entities, matter and mind, to a single one, such that they are merged in the latter, and at the same time a prodigious multiplication of purely mental agents in the world. In other words, it implies both the discontinuity of the elements and the homogeneity of their being. Moreover, it is only on these two conditions that the universe is wholly transparent to the gaze of the intellect. Now, on the one hand, as a result of having been sounded a thousand times and judged unfathomable, the abyss which separates movement and consciousness, object and subject, the mechanical and the logical, has at length been called once more into question, relegated to the status of an appearance, and finally denied altogether by the bravest souls, who have been echoed from every quarter. On the other hand, the progress of chemistry leads us to affirm the atom and to deny the material continuity which the continuous character of the physical and living manifestations of matter, extension, movement and growth

---

1. [Trans. Note: The epigraph references Newton's famous tag *'hypotheses non fingo'* (I make no hypotheses), in the *General Scholium* to the *Principia Mathematica*.]

seem superficially to reveal. There is nothing more profoundly surprising than the combination of chemical substances in definite proportions, to the exclusion of any intermediate proportion. Here there is no evolution and no transition: the dividing lines are clear and stark; and yet hence arises everything which is supple and harmoniously graduated in phenomena, almost as if the continuity of nuances were impossible without the discontinuity of colours. The path of chemistry is not the only one which seems to lead us in its progress to the monads; so too do physics, the natural sciences, history, and even mathematics. As Lange says: 'Of great importance, not only for this demonstration, but also especially for its far-reaching consequences, was Newton's assumption that the gravitation of a planet is only the sum of the gravitation of all its individual portions. From this immediately flowed the inference that the terrestrial bodies gravitate towards each other; and further, that even the smallest particles of these masses attract each other'.[2] With this viewpoint, which was much more original than it seems today, Newton broke, and indeed pulverized the individuality of the celestial body, which had until then been regarded as a superior unity whose internal relations bore no resemblance to its relations with other bodies. Great strength of mind was required to resolve this apparent unity into a multiplicity of distinct elements linked to each other in the same way as they are linked to the elements of other aggregates. The beginning of the progress of physics and astronomy can be dated to the day when this viewpoint replaced the contrary prejudice.

In this respect the founders of cellular theory have shown themselves to be Newton's true heirs. In the same way they have broken apart the unity of the living body, they have resolved it into a prodigious number of elementary organisms, isolated and egoistic, eager (*avides*) to develop themselves at the expense of the exterior, where the exterior includes their neighbouring brother cells as well as the inorganic particles of air, water, and all other substances. Schwann's[3] position on this point has been no less fertile than Newton's. Thanks to his cellular theory, we know that 'there is no vital force, as a principle distinct from matter, either

---

2. [Trans. Note: Ludwig Lange (1863-1936), *History of Materialism: And Criticism of its Present Importance*, vol. I, trans. E. C. Thomas, London, Kegan Paul, Trench, Trübner, 1925, p. 311.]

3. [Trans. Note: Theodor Schwann (1810-1882) was one of the key early proponents of the theory that all living organisms are made up of cells.]

in the entirety of the organism, or in each cell. *All phenomena of vegetable or animal life must be explained by the properties of atoms* [let us say of the ultimate elements from which atoms are composed], *whether these be the known forces of inert nature or forces hitherto unknown*.[4] There is surely nothing more positivist or better conformed to a healthy and serious science than this radical negation of the vital principle, against which vulgar spiritualism likes to protest. However, it is clear where this tendency will lead us, if drawn to its logical conclusion: to the monads, which fulfil the most daring promises of Leibnizian spiritualism. Like the vital principle, illness, which was treated as a person by the ancient medical writers, has been pulverized into a great number of infinitesimal disorders of the histological elements. Moreover, thanks primarily to the discoveries of Pasteur, the parasitic theory of illness, which explains these disorders by means of the internal conflicts of miniscule organisms, finds more general application every day, and indeed excessively so, to the point where it should provoke some reaction. But parasites, too, have their parasites. And so on. The infinitesimal again!

The new theories in chemistry have been formed along analogous lines. As Wurtz says: 'This is the new and essential point. *The properties of the radicals are referred to the elements themselves.* Formerly they were considered as a whole. To the radical regarded as a whole was attributed the power of combining with or of being substituted for simple bodies. This was the fundamental point of view of Gerhardt's theory of types. We now go further. To discover and define the properties of radicals we go back to the atoms of which they are composed'.[5] This eminent chemist's thought goes further than our remarks above. The examples which he cites demonstrate that, among the atoms of a radical, there is one in particular on whose atomicity and as yet unsatisfied avidity, outlasting the saturation of all the others, the combination which is produced ultimately depends.

Like stars, like living things, like illnesses, like chemical radicals, nations are nothing more than entities which have long been

---

4. [Trans. Note: These two sentences are marked as a citation in the text, but appear to be not a verbatim quote but a summary paraphrase of the final section ('Theory of the Cells') of T. Schwann, *Microscopical researches into the accordance in the structure and growth of animals and plants*, trans. H. Smith, London, Sydenham Society, 1847.]

5. [Trans. Note: A. Wurtz, *The Atomic Theory*, trans. E. Cleminshaw, London, Kegan Paul, 1880, pp. 265-266 (Tarde's emphasis).]

taken for true beings in the ambitious and sterile theories of so-called philosophical historians. Has it not, for example, been sufficiently repeated that it is foolish to seek the cause of a political or social revolution in the influence of writers, of statesmen, or of any kind of instigator, and that it rather springs spontaneously from the genius of the race, from the bowels of the people, that anonymous and superhuman agent? But this convenient point of view, which consists in mistakenly seeing the creation of a new being in a phenomenon generated by the encounter of real beings (albeit a genuinely new and unforeseen phenomenon), can be upheld only provisionally. Having been rapidly exhausted by the literary abuses it has suffered, it is conducive to a serious return towards a clearer and more positive form of explanation, which accounts for a given historical event only by individual actions, and particularly by the action of inventive men who served as a model for others and reproduced thousands of copies of themselves, like mother-cells of the social body.

This is not all: these ultimate elements which form the final stage of every science, the social individual, the living cell, the chemical atom, are ultimate only from the point of view of their particular science. They themselves, as we know, are composite, not excepting the atom itself which, according to Thomson's hypothesis of the 'vortex atom',[6] the most plausible or the least unacceptable of the conjectures which have been attempted on this subject, would be a whirling mass of simpler elements. Lockyer's[7] studies of solar and stellar spectra have led him to suppose—and the conjecture seems probable—that certain *weak lines* observed by him are due to the elements of which are composed certain substances that on our planet are regarded as incomposite.

Scientists who live in daily contact with the so-called elements have no doubt of their complexity. While Wurtz shows himself to be favourable to Thomson's hypothesis, Berthelot says for his part: 'The deeper study of the elementary masses which, on our current understanding, constitute the simple bodies leads every day more and more to an understanding of them not as indivisible atoms, homogenous and admitting of movement only as a whole,

6. [Trans. Note: J. J. Thomson's 'nebular' or 'vortex atom' theory, prior to the discovery of the electron, posited that the atom consisted of nebular 'vortices' in the ether. As of the writing of *Monadology and Sociology*, little was known of the internal structure of the atom.]

7. [Trans. Note: Norman Lockyer (1836-1920), astronomer and pioneer of astronomical spectroscopy.]

but as *highly complex* constructions, furnished with a specific architecture and animated by *highly varied internal movements*.[8] Physiologists, for their part, do not maintain that the protoplasm is a homogenous substance, and judge only the solid part of the cell to be active and truly living. The soluble part, almost in its entirety, is nothing but a storehouse for fuel and nourishment (or a mass of excrement). Moreover, a better understanding of the solid part itself would doubtless lead us to eliminate almost everything from it. And, where will this process of elimination finish if not at a geometrical point, that is, at pure nothingness? Unless, as we will explain below, this point is a centre. And, in fact, in the true histological element (which is designated only improperly by the word 'cell') what it is essential to take into account is not its limit or envelope, but rather the central focus whence it seems to aspire to radiate indefinitely until the day when the cruel experience of external obstacles obliges it to close in on itself in order to preserve its being; but we are getting ahead of ourselves.

There is no way to call a halt to this descent to the infinitesimal, which, most unexpectedly, becomes the key to the entire universe. This may explain the growing importance of the infinitesimal calculus; and, for the same reason, the stunning and rapid success of the theory of evolution. In this theory, a specific form is, as a geometer would say, the integral of innumerable differentials called individual variations, which are themselves due to cellular variations, whose basis consists of a myriad of elementary changes. The source, reason, and ground of the finite and separate is in the infinitely small, in the imperceptible: this is the profound conviction which inspired Leibniz, and continues to inspire our transformists.

But why should such a transformation, which is incomprehensible if presented as a sum of definite and discrete differences, be readily understood if we consider it as a sum of infinitely small differences? We must show first of all that this is a real contrast. Suppose that, by some miracle, a body disappears and is annihilated from the place A where it was, then appears and *comes back into being* at the place Z a metre away from A, *without having traversed the intermediate positions*: such a *displacement* is beyond the power of our mind to grasp, while we would never be astonished to see this body move from A to Z along a line of juxtaposed positions.

---

8. [Trans. Note: Marcellin Berthelot (1827-1907), chemist. The citation has not been traced.]

However, note that in the first case, we would have been *no less* amazed had we seen such an abrupt disappearance and reappearance take place over a distance of half a metre, or of 30, of 20, of 10, of 2 centimetres, or of any perceptible fraction of a millimetre. Our reason, if not our imagination, would be just as struck in the last case as in the original example. In the same way, if we are presented with two distinct living species, be they very distant or closely related, a fungus and a labiate herb, or two herbs of the same genus, in neither case will it be comprehensible that one could suddenly and with no transition turn into the other. But, if we were to be told that by hybridization the fertilized ovule of the one had undergone a deviation, extremely slight at first and then gradually increasing, from its habitual pathway, we would have no difficulty in accepting this. It will be argued that the inconceivability of the first hypothesis is due to a prejudice which has been formed in us by the association of ideas. Nothing could be truer, and precisely this proves that reality, the source of the experience which gave birth to this prejudice, conforms to the explanation of the finite by the infinitesimal. For pure reason, and still more reason *alone*, would never have guessed at this hypothesis; it would even, perhaps, be more inclined to see in the large the source of the small than in the small the source of the large, and it would gladly believe in divine forms which are complete *ab initio*, which could envelop a clod of earth all at once and penetrate it from the outside to the inside. It would even willingly agree with Agassiz[9] that, from the outset, trees have been forests, bees hives, men nations. Science has been able to eliminate this point of view only by the rebellion of contrary facts. To mention only the most obvious, it is the case that an immense sphere of light spread through space is due to the unique vibration, multiplied by contagion, of one central atom of ether,[10]—that the entire population of a species originates from the prodigious multiplication of one unique first ovulary cell, in a kind of generative radiation,—that the presence of the correct astronomical theory in millions of human brains is due to the multiplied repetition of an idea which appeared one day in a cerebral cell of Newton's brain. But, once more, what follows

9. [Trans. Note: Louis Agassiz (1807-1873), palaeontologist. Tarde's reference is to Agassiz' defence of special creation—the position that animal species and human 'races' were separately created by God—and of the fixity and unchangeability of the species thus created.]

10. [Trans. Note: The ether, in the physics of Tarde's time, is the all-pervading substance which serves as the medium through which light propagates.]

from this? *If the infinitesimal differed from the finite only by degree,* if at the basis of things as at their perceptible surface there existed only positions, distances, and displacements, why would a displacement which is inconceivable in the finite realm change its nature in becoming infinitesimal? The infinitesimal, therefore, is qualitatively different from the finite; movement has a cause distinct from itself; being is not exhausted by what appears in phenomena. Everything comes from the infinitesimal and everything returns to it; nothing in the sphere of the finite and complex—a surprising fact which nobody is surprised at—appears suddenly, nor dies away. What should we conclude from this, if not that the infinitely small, in other words the element, is the source and the goal, the substance and the reason of all things?—While the progress of physics leads physicists to *quantify* nature in order to understand it, it is remarkable that the progress of mathematics leads mathematicians, in order to understand quantity, to resolve it into elements which are not at all quantitative.[11]

This growing importance which the growth of knowledge grants to the concept of the infinitesimal is all the more curious since the latter, in its ordinary form (leaving aside for a moment the monadic hypothesis), is nothing but a mass of contradictions. I will leave to Renouvier[12] the task of pointing them out. By what power could the absurd grant to the human mind the key to the world? Is it not because, through this purely negative concept, we aim at but do not reach, or look at but do not see, a much more positive concept which we do not own, but which should nonetheless be inscribed *as a reminder* in the inventory of our intellectual assets? This absurdity could very well be only the outer covering of a reality alien to everything we know, outside everything, space and time, matter and mind ... Outside mind? If so, the monadic hypothesis should be rejected ... but this must be examined further. However this question is resolved, these tiny beings which we call infinitesimal will be the real *agents*, and these tiny variations which we call infinitesimal will be the real *actions*.

Indeed, it seems to follow from the preceding that these agents are autonomous, and that these variations clash and obstruct one

11. [Trans. Note: Tarde may be thinking here of the work of Georg Cantor and Richard Dedekind in the 1870s and 1880s on the set-theoretical foundations of natural number.]

12. [Trans. Note: Charles Renouvier (1815-1903), philosopher. Renouvier strongly criticized the concepts of infinite and infinitesimal magnitude as logically contradictory.]

another as much as they compete. If everything comes from the infinitesimal, it is because an element, a unique element, initiates some change, movement, vital evolution, or mental or social transformation. If all these changes are gradual and apparently continuous, this shows that the initiative undertaken by the element, even if it receives some support, has also encountered some resistance. Let us imagine that all the citizens of a State, without exception, are fully in favour of a programme of political reorganization springing from the brain of one among their number, and more particularly from one point within this brain; the complete overhaul of the State according to this plan, rather than being progressive and fragmentary, will then be abrupt and total, however radical the project. The slowness of social modifications is explained only by the fact that the other plans for reform or ideals of the State which all other members of a nation knowingly or unknowingly entertain run contrary to this plan. In the same way, if matter were as inert and passive as is generally believed, I do not see why movement, in other words gradual displacement, should exist, nor why the formation of an organism should be subject to the progress of its embryonic phases, an obstacle opposed to the immediate realization of its adult stage which was nonetheless from the beginning the aim of the germ's impulse.

The idea of the straight line, let it be noted, is not the exclusive property of geometry. There is a biological rectilinearity and a logical rectilinearity. In the same way that, in passing from one point to another, the abbreviation or diminution of the number of intervening points cannot continue indefinitely and must stop at the limit which we call the straight line, just so, in the passage from one specific form to another, from an individual state to another, there is a *minimal*, irreducible intervening series of forms or states which must be traversed, which alone may perhaps explain the abbreviated repetition by the embryo of some of the successive forms of its ancestors; and similarly, in expounding a body of knowledge, is there not a way to go *straight* from one thesis to the next, and does it not consist in linking them by a chain of *logical positions* or positings which necessarily come in between the two? A truly surprising necessity. This rational, rectilinear order of exposition, much favoured by introductory books which summarize in a few pages the labour of centuries (and the limit of the ambition of such volumes), coincides frequently but not invariably, and in many points but not in all, with the historical order of appearance of the successive discoveries which are synthesized in the science. Perhaps this is the case with the famous recapitulation of *phylogeny* by *ontogeny*,[13] which would then be the rectification and not only the prodigious acceleration of the more or less winding path along which the ancestral forms, the accumulated *biological inventions* which are bequeathed all together to the ovule, followed one another in previous eras.[14]

The real support which the theory of evolution gives to the monadological hypotheses will be still more evident if we imagine this great system in the new forms which it will soon take on, and whose outline can already be seen. For evolutionary theory itself evolves. It evolves not by a series or a competition of blind groupings, or of fortuitous and involuntary adaptations to the observed facts, in conformity with the procedures of transformation which it wrongly attributes to living nature, but by the accumulated efforts of perfectly aware scientists and theoreticians, knowingly and voluntarily occupied in modifying the fundamental theory to fit it as closely as possible to the scientific data known to them, and also to the preconceived ideas they hold dear. This theory is for them a *generic form* which they are working to *specify*, each in his own way. But, among these various products of the unprecedented fermentation created by Darwin, there are only two which add to or substitute for the master's own idea something truly new and fertile. I refer firstly to the *evolution by association* of elementary organisms into more complex organisms formulated by Edmond Perrier,[15] and secondly by the *evolution by leaps* or crises,[16] which, suggested and predicted some years ago by Cornet's prescient writings,[17]

13. [Trans. Note: Reading *ontogenèse* with the 1893 text; the 1895 text has *autogenèse* (autogeny).]

14. [Trans. Note: The theory of ontogenetic recapitulation, most famously formulated by Ernst Haeckel (1834-1919) as 'ontogeny recapitulates phylogeny', holds that the developing embryo 'recapitulates' in miniature the evolution of the species.]

15. [Trans. Note: Edmond Perrier (1844-1921), zoologist. As described by Tarde, Perrier propounded the theory that higher organisms evolved from colonies or associations of smaller organisms. See E. Perrier, *Les Colonies animales et la formation des organismes*, Paris, Masson, 1881. The 1893 text cites Perrier's courses at the Museum (the National Museum of Natural History in Paris) and adds the following footnote: 'This biological theory has the advantage that it agrees in every point with the linguistic theory of the formation of languages by the aggregation of several words into one'.]

16. [Trans. Note: The 1893 text adds the English phrase 'saltatory evolution'.]

17. [Trans. Note: Antoine Augustin Cournot (1801-1877), mathematician, economist and philosopher. See his *Traité de l'enchaînement des idées fondamentales*,

has spontaneously sprouted anew[18] here and there in the minds of several contemporary scientists. The specific transformation of a pre-existing form in view of a new adaptation, according to one of these theorists, must have come about *at a given moment in a quasi-immediate manner* (that is, I think, very short relative to the prodigious duration of species once they are formed, but perhaps very long with respect to our brief existence) and, he adds, by a *regular process* and not by groping its way forward. Similarly, for another transformist, the species, from its relatively rapid formation up to its equally rapid decomposition, actually remains fixed within certain limits, because it is essentially in a state of stable organic equilibrium. Deeply troubled in its own constitution by any excessive change in its environment (or by any internal revolution due to the contagious rebellion of an element) the organism goes beyond its species only, as it were, to roll onto the slope of another species, itself in stable equilibrium, and there remains for some period of time which for us would be an eternity.

Of course, I need not here discuss these conjectures. It is sufficient to note that they are growing, or rather advancing through the undergrowth, still lowly but pervasive, while natural selection loses ground every day, showing itself better at purifying forms than perfecting them, and better at perfecting them than fundamentally modifying them. I would add that, by the one or the other of the two ways mentioned above, we are necessarily led to populate and fill living bodies with spiritual or quasi-spiritual atoms. To what may we ascribe the *need for society* which Perrier sees as the soul of the organic world, if not to tiny *persons*? And what could this transformation be, this *direct, regular,* and rapid process imagined by other thinkers, if not the accomplishment

---

section III.8, *Œuvres complètes*, Vol. III, N. Bruyère (ed.), Paris, Vrin, 1982, pp. 267-277.]

18. [Trans. Note: The 1893 text adds: '... sprouted anew at once in the mind of two contemporary scientist, both avowed transformists. By one of those coincidences which often occur in the history of science, and which invariably denote the full maturity of an idea whose hour has come and which imperiously demands attention, the latter of the above-mentioned hypotheses, published in 1877 by the American naturalist Dall, was presented in 1879 at the scientific section of the Academy of Brussels by the Belgian scientist de Sélys Longchamps as his own discovery'. The idea in the next sentence is credited to de Sélys Longchamps (Michel-Edmond de Sélys Longchamps (1813-1900), naturalist) and in the sentence following ('another transformist') to Dall (William Healey Dall (1845-1927), naturalist). See W. H. Dall (1877) On a provisional hypothesis of saltatory evolution. *American Naturalist*, vol. 11, no. 3, pp. 135-137.]

of hidden workers who collaborate in realizing some *specific plan for reorganization* previously conceived and willed by one among their number?

II

This should, I think, suffice to demonstrate how science tends to pulverize the universe and to multiply beings indefinitely. However, as already noted, science tends no less distinctly to unify the Cartesian duality of matter and mind. Hence it is inevitably led to, let us say not anthropomorphism, but *psychomorphism*. Monism can effectively be conceived in three ways (I am of course aware that this has been said many times before): either by seeing movement and consciousness—for example the vibration of a cerebral cell and the corresponding mental state—as two *sides* of a single fact, in which case one misleads oneself by this reminder of the ancient Janus; or by not denying the heterogeneous nature of matter and mind, but making them flow from a common source, from a hidden and unknown mind, a position which gains nothing but a trinity instead of, and in the place of, a duality: or, finally, by holding resolutely that matter is mind, nothing more. This last thesis is the only comprehensible one, and the only one which truly leads to the desired reduction. But there are two ways in which it may be understood. We may say with the idealists that the material universe, other egos included, is *mine*, exclusively mine, and that it is composed of my states of mind or of their possibility to the extent that it is affirmed by me, that is, to the extent that this possibility is itself one of my states of mind. If this interpretation be rejected, the only option is to admit with the monadologists that the whole external universe is composed of souls distinct from my own but fundamentally similar. In accepting this latter point of view, it so happens that one removes from the former its best support. To recognize that one knows nothing of *the being in itself of a stone* or a plant, say, and at the same time to stubbornly persist in saying that it *is*, is logically untenable; the idea which we have of it, as may easily be shown, has for its only content our states of mind; and as, abstracting away our states of mind, nothing remains, either it is only these states of mind which are affirmed when we affirm this substantial and unknowable X, or it must be admitted that in affirming some other thing, we affirm nothing. But if it is the case that this being in itself is fundamentally similar to our own being, then it will no longer be unknowable, and may consistently be affirmed.

Thus monism leads us to universal psychomorphism. Hitherto, however, monism has been demonstrated less than it has been affirmed. It is true that when one sees physicists like Tyndall, naturalists like Haeckel, philosophical historians and artists like Taine, and theorists of all schools,[19] express the suspicion or the conviction that the hiatus between inside and outside, between sensation and vibration, is an illusion, then even if their arguments may not be convincing, the agreement of their convictions and presentiments has some importance. But, as soon as they attempt to put their finger on the alleged identity, this presumption loses all force in the face of the evident discord of the juxtaposed terms which they are trying to identify, namely *movement* and *sensation*.

The reason is that at least one of these terms is an unfortunate choice. The contrast between the purely quantitative variations of movement, whose deviations are themselves measurable, and the purely qualitative variations of sensation, whether they concern colours, odors, tastes or sounds, is too shocking to our mind. But if, among our internal states, distinct *ex hypothesi* from sensation, there were to be found some which vary quantitatively, as I have attempted to show elsewhere,[20] this singular character would perhaps allow us to attempt to use them to *spiritualize* the universe. In my view, these two states of the soul, or rather these two forces of the soul which are called belief and desire, whence derive *affirmation* and *will*, present this character eminently and distinctly. By the universality of their presence in all psychological phenomena, both human and animal, by the homogeneity of their nature from

19. [Trans. Note: John Tyndall (1820-1893), physicist; Ernst Haeckel (1834-1919), biologist and naturalist; Hippolyte Taine (1828-1893), historian and literary critic. All argued for some form of dual-aspect monism, in which mind and matter are seen as two aspects of a single underlying reality. Tyndall, sometimes remembered as a thoroughgoing materialist, also seriously considered the idea of a 'primeval union between spirit and matter', such that they would be 'two opposite faces of the self-same mystery' ('Scientific Use of the Imagination' (1870), in *Fragments of Science*, London, Longmans, Green & Co., 1879, vol. II, pp. 101-136, on p. 133). Haeckel propounded a monism which 'recognizes one sole substance in the universe, which is at once "God and nature"; body and spirit (or matter and energy) it holds to be inseparable' (*The Riddle of the Universe*, trans. J. McCabe, London, Watts & Co., 1929, p. 16). Taine, finally, describes mind and matter as 'one and the same tongue, written in different characters' (*On Intelligence*, trans. T. D. Haye, London, L. Reeve & Co., 1871, pp.297-8.)]

20. [Trans. Note: The theory of belief and desire as psychological quantities goes back to Tarde's early (1880) essay 'La Croyance et le désir' ('Belief and desire', in *Essais et mélanges sociologiques*); see particularly section II.]

one end of their immense gamut to the other, from the slightest inclination to believe or to want up to certainty and passion, and finally by their mutual penetration and by other no less striking signs of similarity, belief and desire play exactly the same role in the ego, with respect to sensations, as do space and time in the external world with respect to material elements. It remains to be examined whether this analogy does not conceal an identity, and whether, rather than being simply forms of our sensory experience, as their most profound analyst believed,[21] space and time are not perhaps primitive concepts or continuous and original quasi-sensations by which, thanks to our two faculties of belief and desire, which are the common source of all judgements and hence of all concepts, the degrees and modes of belief and of desire of psychic agents other than ourselves are translated to us. On this hypothesis, the movement of bodies would be nothing other than types of judgements or objectives formulated by the monads.[22]

It will be seen that if this were the case, the universe would become perfectly transparent, and the open conflict between two opposing currents of contemporary science would be resolved. For if, on the one hand, science leads us towards vegetal psychology, to 'cellular psychology', and soon to atomic psychology, in a word to an entirely spiritual interpretation of the mechanical and material world, on the other hand its tendency to explain everything, including thought, in mechanical terms is no less evident. In Haeckel's 'cellular psychology',[23] it is curious to see the alternation

---

21. [Trans. Note: The reference is to Kant's theory of space and time as 'pure forms of intuition' in the Transcendental Aesthetic of the *Critique of Pure Reason*. Tarde speaks slightly loosely here, as Kant regards time as a form of inner as well as outer (sensory) intuition.]

22. According to Lotze, if there is anything spiritual in the atom, this must be pleasure and pain, rather than a concept; I maintain exactly the contrary. [Trans. Note: 'If there is anything spiritual in an atom of material mass, we need not suppose that it has any concept (*Vorstellung*) of its position in the world, or that the powers it exercises are accompanied by any effort (*Strebung*); but we may affirm that it inwardly perceives the pressure or shock, the dilation or contraction which it undergoes in the form of a feeling of pleasure or pain'. (H. Lotze, *Medicinische Psychologie oder Physiologie der Seele*, Leipzig, Weidmann'sche Buchhandlung, 1852, p. 134 = *Principes généraux de psychologie physiologique*, trans. A Penjon, Paris, G. Baillière & Cie, 1881, p. 133.]

23. [Trans. Note: For a brief statement of Haeckel's 'cellular psychology', see his *The Riddle of the Universe* (1899), trans. J. McCabe, London, Watts & Co., 1929, p. 145: 'Just as we take the living cell to be the "elementary organism" in anatomy and physiology, and derive the multicellular animal or plant from it, so, with equal right, we may consider the "cell-soul" to be the psychological unit, and the

of these two contradictory viewpoints between one line and the next. But the contradiction is resolved by the hypothesis set out above, and can only be resolved thus.

Moreover, this hypothesis is in no way anthropomorphic. Belief and desire have the unique privilege of including unconscious states. There certainly exist unconscious desires and judgements. These include, for example, the desires implicit in our pleasures and pains, and the judgements of localization and so on which are incorporated in our sensations. By contrast, unconscious and unfelt sensations are a manifest impossibility; if a few minds have thought to posit them, it is either because they have used this phrase mistakenly to refer to sensations which are not affirmed or discerned, or because, while understanding that it is really necessary to admit unconscious states of mind, they have wrongly understood sensations as capable of being such states. In addition, the facts which have been used to support the hypothesis of unconscious sensibility, already striking enough in themselves, also serve to prove general conclusions considerably beyond this. They show that our own consciousness (that is, the directing monads or leading elements of the brain) has as its constant and indispensable collaborators innumerable other consciousnesses whose modifications, external with respect to us, are for them internal states. Ball says: 'Certain physiologists who take an interest in psychology have proved that we cannot forget anything. Traces of our previously received impressions accumulate in the cells of our brains, where they remain latent indefinitely, until one day a superior influence awakens them from the tomb where they were buried in sleep ... When in the course of a conversation one tries to remember a name, a date, or a fact, the information sought often escapes us, and only several hours later, when we are thinking of something else entirely, does it come spontaneously to offer itself to us. How can we explain this unexpected revelation? It is because a *mysterious secretary*, a skilful automaton has been *working for us while the intellect* [he should have said *our* own intellect, the directing monad] neglects these trivial details'.[24]

---

complex psychic activity of the higher organism to be the result of the psychic activity of the cells which compose it' For a more in-depth exposition, see *Zellseelen und Seelenzellen*, Leipzig, Alfred Kröner Verlag, 1909.]

24. [Trans. Note: Probably Benjamin Ball (1833-1893), psychologist. The citation has not been traced.]

That psychiatrists find it necessary to have recourse to the metaphors of a *secretary* or an interior *librarian* to explain the phenomena of memory, constitutes a strong presumption in favour of the monadic hypothesis. The monadological theory can therefore readily appropriate for itself the arguments of the English and German psychologists on this subject. But since, after all, it seems to be necessary to see as unconscious in some cases some states of mind, let it be noted that in truth, a desire or an act of faith not only can exist without being felt, but actually cannot be felt as such, any more than a sensation can be active by itself. Now, by this remarkable characteristic, the two internal forces I have named are distinguished for us by being objectifiable (*objectivable*) to the highest degree. Since they may apply to any sensation whatsoever, however radically different these sensations may be from each other, to the colour red as to the note C or D, to the smell of a rose as to the feeling of cold or warmth, why may they not apply just as much to *unknown* and, I submit, unknowable phenomena, *ex hypothesi* different from sensations, but no more or less distinct from sensations than the latter are from each other? Why may *sensation* not be seen simply as a species of the genus *quality*, and may not one admit that there exist outside us *non-sensory qualifying signs* which, just like our sensations, may serve as the point of application for the psychic forces *par excellence*, namely the static force called belief and the dynamic force called desire? It is perhaps from an instinctive and confused feeling of this truth that the idea of force has been built on the model of desire, and the key to the universal enigma sought in this idea. Schopenhauer lifted the mask of this concept by calling it almost by its true name, will. But will is a combination of faith and desire, and the master's disciples, Hartmann among them, had to add the idea to the will.[25] They would have done better to break apart the will and distinguish in it the two elements. We may rightly be amazed that, among so many philosophical conjectures, it has occurred to nobody, at least explicitly, to seek in the objectification of *belief* rather than of desire the solution to the problems of physics and of life. At least explicitly; for without knowing it, we conceive of matter—coherent and solid substance, satisfied and at rest—not only with the help of, but in the image and likeness of our *convictions*, as we conceive of

---

25. [Trans. Note: Eduard von Hartmann (1842-1906), philosopher. Where Schopenhauer based his thought on a strict separation of will and idea, Hartmann identified the two as dimensions of the unconscious.]

force in the image of our efforts. Only Hegel glimpsed this truth, to judge by his conceit of composing the world from sequences of affirmations and negations. Hence perhaps, despite certain aberrations and strange subtleties, comes the air of architectural and magisterial grandeur which pervades his ruined work, and which marks, in general, the superiority of substantialist systems throughout history, from Democritus to Descartes, over the liveliest of dynamistic doctrines. Have we not seen monism, beneath the brilliant light of the currently prevailing evolutionism, which pushes to its limit the Leibnizian idea of force, attempting the renewal of the Spinozan concept of substance? For, as will moves towards certitude, as the movement of stars and atoms moves towards their definitive agglomeration, the idea of force leads naturally to the idea of substance, where, weary of the agitations of an illusory phenomenalism, grasping finally realities which are taken for immutable, idealist and materialist thought each in turn take refuge. But, of these two ascriptions to the mysterious external noumena of our two interior quantities, which is legitimate? Why may we not dare to say that both are?

It will perhaps be objected that this *psychomorphism* is a very easy solution, and all the more illusory for that, and that it is a delusion to pretend that one can explain vital, physical or chemical phenomena by psychological facts, since the latter are always more complex than the former. But, though I admit the complexity of sensations and the complete legitimacy of explaining them by physiological facts, I cannot admit this of desire nor of belief. I maintain that analysis cannot get its teeth into these irreducible concepts. There is an unnoticed contradiction in the position that, on the one hand, an organism is a mechanism constructed in conformity to purely mechanical laws, and, on the other, that all the phenomena of mental life, including the two mentioned above, are purely products of the organization created by this life, and do not exist prior to it. If, in fact, the organized being is only an admirably constructed machine, it should function like any other machine, in which not only no new force but not even any radically new product can possibly be created by the most marvellous arrangements of wheels and cogs. A machine is nothing but a special distribution and direction of pre-existing forces which traverse it without essentially altering it. It is nothing but a change of form of raw materials which it receives from outside and whose essence does not change. If then, once more, living bodies are machines, the essential nature of those products and those forces which result from their functioning which are known to us fundamentally (sensations, thoughts, volitions) attests that the substances which nourish them (carbon, nitrogen, oxygen, hydrogen etc.) contain hidden psychic elements. In particular, among these superior results of the vital functions, there are two which are forces, and which, springing forth from the brain, could not have been created there by the mechanical play of cellular vibrations. Can it be denied that desire and belief are forces? Is it not clear that with their reciprocal combinations, passions and intentions, they are the perpetual winds of history's tempests, and the waterfalls which turn the mills of politics? What leads the world on and drives it in its course, if not beliefs religious or otherwise, ambitions and cupidities? These so-called products are forces to such an extent that they alone can produce societies, which many contemporary philosophers still maintain are true organisms. The products of an inferior organism would then be factors of a superior organization! Thus, in admitting the dynamical character of these two states of mind, the conclusion (which in any case cannot be escaped by regarding them as products) acquires a higher degree of rigour. For we know that the forces employed by machines always emerge from them considerably less denatured than their raw materials. It follows that, if belief and desire are forces, it is probable that when they *emerge* from the body in our mental manifestations, they do not differ noticeably from how they were when they *entered*, in the form of molecular cohesions or affinities. The ultimate foundation of material substance would then be open to us; and it is worth the trouble of examining whether, in following through the consequences of this point of view, we remain in agreement with the facts established by science. And here I have the advantage of being able to rely on the accumulated work of Schopenhauer, Hartmann and their school, who have, I believe, succeeded in showing the primordial and universal character, not of will, but of desire.

To cite only one example, consider a small mass of protoplasm, in which no sign of organization has been discovered, 'a clear jelly like the white of an egg', as Perrier says. This jelly nonetheless, he adds, executes movements, *captures animalcules, digests them*, etc. It evidently has appetite, and consequently must have a more or less clear perception of what its appetite is for. If desire and belief are nothing but products of organization, whence comes this perception and this appetite of an admittedly heterogeneous, but not yet organized, mass? Almann, of the Royal Society of London, says: 'The movements of spores seem frequently to obey a real *volition*; if the spore encounters an obstacle, it changes direction *and moves back by changing the movement of its cilia*'.[26] A railway mechanic could do no better. Nonetheless, this spore is only a cell detached from an immobile and insensible plant, to which we grant no will and no intelligence. But, lo and behold, intelligence and will all of a sudden appear in the daughter cell, even though they exist not at all, even virtually, in the mother cell! Let us rather say that, when it judges best to do so, when it is useful to its goal, to its particular cosmic plan whence proceed all its movements, the vital element reveals and unfolds its hidden resources. At first mixed with an infinity of others in an indivisible lump of protoplasm, at the desired moment it calls a halt to its indivision, it encloses and sequesters itself with a compact group of vassals, it throws up defensive ramparts of calcium; or else it stretches out its flagella like a rower extending his oars, and moves towards its prey. Every body of water contains myriads of these *unicellular* living beings which 'construct for themselves a skeleton ... of concentric spheres as transparent as crystal, and of a perfect symmetry and beauty'. Evidently the *single cell* under consideration could not accomplish these prodigious feats alone, and we must rather conclude that it was only the soul of a whole people of workers. But what expenditure of psychic acts is required by such a task!

In truth, one might justifiably wonder, when one compares to cellular inventions, cellular industries, and cellular arts, as a spring day *exhibits* them to us, our arts, our industries, and our little human discoveries displayed in our periodical exhibitions, whether it is really certain that our own intelligence and will, those great *egos* disposing of the vast resources of a gigantic cerebral state, are superior to those of the tiny egos confined in the miniscule city of an animal or even plant cell. Surely, if we were not blinded by the prejudice of always considering ourselves superior to everything, such comparisons would not be to our advantage. At root, it is this prejudice which prevents us from believing in the monads. In its age-long effort to interpret everything outside us in terms of mechanism, even those things which most break forth with accumulated signs of genius, namely living beings, our mind as it were blows out all the lights of the world for the sole benefit of its own little

---

26. [Trans. Note: George James Almann (1812-1898), botanist and zoologist. The citation has not been traced.]

spark. Certainly Espinas[27] is right to say that *a small amount of intelligence* suffices to explain the social work of bees and ants. But if one grants this *small amount* and judges it necessary to account for the products of these insects—which are in any case very simple, like the products of our industries—it must be admitted that to produce their organization, so infinitely superior in complexity, in richness, and in adaptive flexibility to all their works, *a great deal* of intelligence and many *intelligences* were necessary.—A remark naturally suggests itself at this point: Since the accomplishment of the simplest and most banal social function, which has persisted unchanged over centuries (for example, the reasonably regular co-ordinated movement of a procession or a regiment) demands, as we know, so much preparatory training, so many words, so much effort, and so much mental force spent almost all in vain—then what torrents of mental or quasi-mental energy must be necessary to produce these complex manoeuvres of simultaneously accomplished vital functions, by not thousands but billions of different actors, all of them, we have reason to think, essentially egotistical, and all as different from each other as the citizens of a vast empire!

It would doubtless be necessary to reject this conclusion if it were proven, or had even a modicum of probability, that beyond a certain degree of corporeal smallness, intelligence (I do not mean sensory intelligence as we know it, but *psyche*, the genus of which all intelligence known to us is only a species) was impossible. If this impossibility were established, we could deduce that all psychological phenomena are results radically different from their conditions, even though all intelligent beings observed by us, or more generally all beings which have a psyche, proceed from parents or ancestors who equally have a psyche, and even though the spontaneous generation of intelligence is a hypothesis even less acceptable, if such a thing be possible, than the spontaneous generation of life. But however far we penetrate into the microscopic and even ultra-microscopic depths of the infinitely small, we will always discover living seeds and complete organisms, in which observation or induction will lead us to recognize the characteristics of animality as much as of vegetation, since the two kingdoms are indistinguishable *in minimis*. As Spottiswoode says: 'A diameter

---

27. [Trans. Note: Alfred Espinas (1844-1922), sociologist. The reference is to his work *Des Sociétés animales [Animal Societies]*, Paris, G. Baillière, 1877. In fact, Espinas' own view of the scope of intelligence in social insects is closer to Tarde's than the text may suggest.]

of 1/3000 millimetres is approximately the smallest that a microscope allows us to see distinctly. But solar rays and electric light reveal to us the presence of bodies *infinitely beneath* these dimensions. Tyndall had the idea of measuring them as a function of light waves ... by observing a mass of them and noting the hues they reflected ... These infinitely small bodies are not just gaseous molecules; they include moreover *complete organisms*, and the illustrious scientist just cited has made a thorough study of the considerable influence which these miniscule organisms exercise in the economy of life'.[28]

But, it will be objected, even if we cannot thus attain the limits of the psychic, nonetheless common sense affirms that, by and large, beings much smaller than ourselves are much less intelligent; and, following this progression, we are sure to arrive, on the path of increasing smallness, at the absolute absence of intelligence. Common sense indeed! Common sense also tells us that intelligence is incompatible with excessive size and in this, it must be admitted, experience proves it right. But if we juxtapose these two commonsensical affirmations, the one unmotivated, the other likely, it is clear that they emerge from the prejudice of anthropocentrism. In reality, we judge beings to be less intelligent the less we understand them, and the error of thinking the unknown to be unintelligent goes hand in hand with the error, which we will examine below,[29] of thinking the unknown to be indistinct, undifferentiated, and homogenous.

The foregoing should on no account be seen as a disguised plea in favour of the teleological principle (*principe de finalité*), which is now so rightly discredited in its ordinary form. Perhaps, in fact, from a methodological point of view, it would be preferable to deny nature any goal and any idea than to claim, as many do, that all her goals and all her ideas can be linked to a single thought and will. This would be a curious way to explain a world where beings are constantly devouring each other; where, in each being, the agreement of functions, to the extent that it exists at all, is nothing but a transaction of contrary interests and claims; where in the normal state, and in the most balanced individual, useless functions and organs can be seen, in the same way as in the best-governed State dissident sects will always spring up, and provincial particularities

---

28. [Trans. Note: William Spottiswoode (1825-1883), mathematician and physicist. The citation has not been traced.]

29. [Trans. Note: See chapter VI below.]

will be religiously perpetuated by the citizens and of necessity respected by the rulers, even though they disrupt the unity which is their dream! However infinite one may suppose thought or divine will to be, if it is to be *one* thing, it will *ipso facto* become inadequate as an explanation of reality. Between its infinity, which supposes the coexistence of contradictories, and its unity, which demands perfect agreement, we must choose,—or else make, in a marvellous fashion, the one proceed from the other, each in turn, the latter from the former, then the former from the latter ... But let us not become involved with such mysteries. Either there is no intelligence at all in matter, or matter is wholly saturated with intelligence; there is no middle ground. And in truth, scientifically speaking, it comes down to the same thing. Let us suppose for a moment that one of our human States, composed not of a few thousand but of a few *quadrillions* or *quintillions* of men, hermetically sealed and inaccessible as individuals (like China, but infinitely more populous still, and more closed) was known to us only by the data of its statisticians, whose figures, made up of very large numbers, recurred with extreme regularity. When a political or social revolution, which would be revealed to us by an abrupt enlargement or diminution of some of these numbers, took place in this State, we might well be certain that we would be observing a fact caused by individual ideas and passions, but we would resist the temptation to become lost in superfluous conjectures on the nature of these impenetrable causes even though they alone were the real ones, and the wisest option would appear to us to explain as best we could the unusual numbers by ingenious comparisons with clever manipulations of the normal numbers. We would thereby arrive at least at clear results and symbolic truths. Nonetheless, it would be important from time to time to recall the purely symbolic nature of these truths; and precisely this is the service which the theory of monads can offer to science.

III

We have seen that science, having pulverized the universe, necessarily ends up by spiritualizing the dust thus created. However, we now face an important objection. In any monadological or atomistic system, all phenomena are nebulous clouds resolvable into the actions emanating from a multitude of agents who are so many invisible and innumerable little gods. This polytheism— this *myriatheism*, one might almost say—leaves unexplained the universal agreement of phenomena, as imperfect as this may be. If the elements of the world are born separate, independent and autonomous, it is impossible to see why a great number of them and many of the groups formed by them (for example all atoms of oxygen or hydrogen) resemble each other, if not perfectly, as is often supposed without sufficient reason, at least within certain approximately fixed limits; it is impossible to see why many of them, if not all, appear to be captive and subjugated, and to have renounced the absolute liberty which their eternity implies; and finally, it is impossible to see why order and not disorder, and in first place the primary condition of order, namely increasing concentration rather than increasing dispersion, are the result of their relations. Thus it seems necessary to have recourse to new hypotheses. As a complement to the closure of his monads, Leibniz made each one a *camera obscura* where the whole universe of other monads is represented in a reduced form and from a particular angle; and moreover, he had to posit a pre-established harmony, in the same way that, as the complement of their wandering blind atoms, materialists must invoke universal laws or a single formula embracing all laws, a kind of mystical commandment which all beings would obey and which was not produced by any being, a kind of ineffable and unintelligible word which, having never been pronounced by anyone, nonetheless would be heard everywhere and forever. Besides, both atomists and monadologists equally represent their first elements, which they claim are the sources of all reality, as swimming in the same space and the same time, which are two realities or pseudo-realities of a singular kind: deeply penetrating throughout the material realities which were supposed impenetrable, and yet radically distinct from the latter, despite the intimacy of this penetration. All these characteristics are so many mysteries, which create a curious embarrassment for the philosopher. Is there any hope of resolving them by conceiving of open monads which would penetrate each other reciprocally, rather than being mutually external? I believe there is, and I note that on this point again, the progress of science, indeed of modern science in general and not only of its most recent developments, favours the blossoming of a renewed monadology. The Newtonian discovery of gravitation, of action at a distance (and at any distance) of material elements on one another, shows how difficult it will be to make a case for their impenetrability. Each element, hitherto conceived as a point, now becomes an indefinitely enlarged sphere of action (for analogy leads us to believe that gravity, like all other physical forces, is propagated successively);[30] and all these interpenetrating spheres are so many domains proper to each element, so many distinct though intermixed spaces, perhaps, which we wrongly take to be a single unique space. The centre of each sphere is a point, which is uniquely defined by its properties, but in the end a point like any other; and besides, since activity is the very essence of the elements, each of them exists in its entirety in the place where it acts. The atom, in truth, if we draw the implications of this point of view which is naturally suggested by Newton's law (which a few thinkers have occasionally tried, and failed, to explain by the pressure of the ether), ceases to be an atom; it is a *universal medium* [*milieu universel*] or aspires to become one, a universe *in itself*, not only, as Leibniz wished to argue, a *microcosm*, but the entire cosmos vanquished and absorbed by a single being. If, having thus resolved this rather supernatural conception of space into real particular spaces or domains, we could in the same way resolve a single Time, that hollow entity, into multiple realities and elementary desires, then the only remaining simplification would be to explain natural laws, the similarity and repetition of phenomena and the multiplication of similar phenomena (physical waves, living cells, social copies) by the triumph of certain monads who desired these laws, imposed these forms, subjected to their yoke and levelled with their scythe a people of monads thus subjugated and made uniform, although born free and original, all as eager (*avides*) as their conquerors to dominate and assimilate the universe.—Just as much as space and time, natural laws, those equally rootless and fantastical entities, would thus finally find their proper place and their point of application among known realities. They would all have begun, like our civil and political laws, by being the designs and projects of individuals.—Thus we would in the simplest way possible meet the fundamental objection made to any atomistic or monadological attempt to resolve the continuity of phenomena into an elementary discontinuity. *What do we place within the ultimate discontinuity if not continuity?* We place therein, as we will explain again below, the totality of other beings. At the basis of each thing are all real or possible things.

---

30. According to Laplace, the *gravific fluid*, to use his expression, is propagated successively, but with a velocity at least millions of times faster than light. In one place he says 50 million times, in another 100 million.

IV

But this implies first of all that *everything is a society*, that every phenomenon is a social fact. Now, it is remarkable that science, following logically from its preceding tendencies, tends strangely to generalize the concept of society. Science tells us of animal societies (see Espinas' excellent book on this subject[31]), of cellular societies, and why not of atomic societies? I almost forgot to add societies of stars, solar and stellar systems. All sciences seem destined to become branches of sociology. Of course, I am aware that, by a mistaken apprehension of the direction of this current, some have been led to the conclusion that societies are organisms; but the truth is that, since the advent of cellular theory, organisms have on the contrary become societies of a particular kind, fiercely exclusive cities as imagined by a Lycurgus or a Rousseau, or better still, religious congregations of a prodigious tenacity which equals the majestic and invariable strangeness of their rites, an invariability which nonetheless does not count against their individual members' diversity and force of invention.

That a philosopher such as Spencer should assimilate societies to organisms[32] is not surprising, and fundamentally not new, except perhaps for the extraordinary expenditure of imaginative erudition in the service of this view. But it is truly remarkable that a highly circumspect natural scientist such as Edmond Perrier can see in the assimilation of organisms to societies the key to the mysteries of living things and the ultimate formula of evolution. Having said that *'one may compare an animal or a plant to a populous town, in which numerous corporations flourish, and that blood cells are like merchants carrying with them in the liquid wherein they swim the complex baggage which they trade'*, he adds: 'In the same way that we have employed every comparison furnished by the degrees of consanguinity to express the relations of animals to each other, before supposing that they were genuinely related and in effect consanguineous, so the comparisons of organisms to societies and societies to organisms have recurred ceaselessly to the present day, without anyone seeing in these comparisons anything more than forms of expression. *We, on the contrary, have arrived at the conclusion that association played*

---

31. [Trans. Note: See note 27 above.]
32. [Trans. Note: Herbert Spencer (1820-1903), philosopher. See 'The Social Organism' (1860), in *Essays: Scientific, Political and Speculative*, London, Williams and Norgate, 1868, vol. I, pp. 384-428.]

a considerable, if not exclusive role in the gradual development of organisms', and so on.[33]

It should however be noted at this point that science also increasingly assimilates organisms to mechanisms, and that it lowers the barriers previously erected between the living and the inorganic worlds. Why then may the molecule, for example, not be a society just as much as the plant or the animal? The relative regularity and permanence of the apparent opposition between phenomena of a molecular order and phenomena of a cellular or vital order should in no way lead us to reject this conjecture, if, with Cournot, we consider further that human societies pass, in the process of becoming civilized, from a barbaric and as it were *organic* phase to a *physical* and *mechanical* phase. In the first stage, all the general facts of the instinctive development of their genius, in their poetry, their arts, their languages, their customs and their laws, curiously recall the characteristics and processes of life; and thence they pass by degrees to an administrative, industrial, scientific, reasonable, and in a word mechanical phase, which by the great numbers which it has at its disposal, arranged in equal heaps by the statistician, gives rise to the appearance of economic laws or pseudo-laws, which are so analogous in many respects to physical laws, and particularly to the laws of statics. From this similarity, which is supported by a whole mass of facts, and for which I refer the reader to Cournot's *Treatise on the Order of the Fundamental Ideas*,[34] it follows first of all that the chasm between the nature of inorganic beings and the nature of living things is not unbridgeable (contrary to an error which Cournot himself makes on this point), since we see the same evolution, that of our societies, take on alternately the attributes of the latter and those of the former. It follows secondly that if a living thing is a society, *a fortiori* a purely mechanical being must also be one, since the progress of society consists in mechanization. A molecule would then be, compared to an organism or to a State, only a kind of infinitely more numerous and more advanced nation, arrived at the stationary period which J. S. Mill calls forth with all his will.[35]

33. [Trans. Note: For Perrier, see note 15 above. This citation has not been traced (Tarde may be paraphrasing rather than citing exactly).]
34. [Trans. Note: Cournot, *Traité* (note 17), section IV.1 (ed. cited pp. 296-311).]
35. [Trans. Note: See J. S. Mill, 'Of the Stationary State', *Principles of Political Economy*, vol. II, book IV, ch. 6, 5th ed., London, Parker, Son & Bourn, 1862, pp. 320-326.]

Let us move immediately on to the most specious objection yet made to this assimilation of organisms, and *a fortiori* of physical things, to societies. The most striking contrast between nations and living bodies is that living bodies have defined and symmetric contours, while the borders of nations or the walls of cities are drawn on the earth with a capricious irregularity which clearly demonstrates the absence of any pre-ordained plan. Spencer and Espinas have responded in different ways to this difficulty,[36] but, I believe, there is another possible response.

The contrast cannot be denied—it is a very real one—but it admits of a plausible explanation; here I offer a simplified version of this explanation for ease of understanding. Leaving to one side the defined and symmetrical nature of organic forms, let us focus solely on another characteristic linked to the former, namely that the length, breadth and height of an organism are never in extreme disproportion to one another. In snakes and poplar trees, height or length is noticeably greater than the other dimensions; in flatfish the thickness is much less; but, in any case, the disproportion visible in these extreme forms cannot be likened to that consistently displayed by any given social aggregate. Take for example China, which has a length and breadth of 3000 kilometres, but an average height of only 1 or 2 metres, since the Chinese are rather short and their buildings low. Even a mediaeval state consisting of a single fortified town tightly constrained within its defensive walls, and whose houses of several floors overhang the streets, still has a very small thickness compared to its horizontal extension. But does this latter example not put us on the trail of the desired solution? It is in order to better resist external attack that a city is fortified and agglomerated, and that floors mount up; if in modern capitals, where this huddling-up is not imposed by the insecurity of the times, houses still tend to become ever taller, this is for a reason which often conflicts with the preceding, namely to satisfy the need felt by an ever-growing number of men to participate in the social advantages of the greatest possible assembly of people in the smallest possible space. If this lively instinct of sociability which makes men want to agglomerate themselves, either to better defend themselves or to develop themselves more fully, did not

---

36. [Trans. Note: Spencer's and Espinas' responses are in fact broadly similar, and primarily rest on questioning the presumption that the forms of organisms are necessarily well-defined and symmetrical (see e.g. Spencer, 'The Social Organism', edition cited, pp. 393-394; Espinas, *Les Sociétés animales*, pp. 216-217).]

rapidly encounter an impassable limit, it is likely that we would see nations composed of clusters of men towering into the air, supported on the earth without spreading over it. But it is hardly necessary to indicate why this is impossible. A nation which was as high as it was wide would surpass the breathable zone of the earth's atmosphere by a considerable distance, and the earth's crust provides no material sufficiently solid for the titanic constructions demanded by such urban development in a vertical direction. Besides, beyond a height of a few metres, the resulting inconveniences outweigh the advantages, as a result of man's physical makeup, in which all the senses and organs respond exclusively to the demands of horizontal expansion. Man's nature is to walk rather than climb, to see forwards and not up or down, and so on. Finally, the enemies he fears do not fly in the air but wander on the earth. In this light, it would be of no use to a nation to be *very tall*. For cellular aggregates such as animals or plants, the situation is otherwise. They are just as likely to be unexpectedly attacked from above as from the side, and must therefore be prepared to defend themselves in every direction. Moreover, the constitution of the anatomical elements which make up living bodies is nowise limited to co-ordination in the horizontal plane. There is therefore no obstacle to the unlimited satisfaction of the sociable instincts which we see in them.

This said, do we not see that, the more a social aggregate grows in height at the expense of its two other dimensions, and in this respect diminishes the (albeit still considerable) distance which separates it from organic forms, the more it comes to resemble the latter also by its regularity and by the increasing symmetry of its external shape and internal structure? A large public corporation, a government school, a barracks, or a monastery are all so many highly centralized and highly disciplined small States, which confirm this perspective on the facts. Conversely, when an organized being such as a lichen on occasion takes the form of a thin layer of widely spread cells, it will be noted that its contours are ill-defined and asymmetrical.

We may discover the significance of this symmetry which, as a rule, is enjoyed by living forms, by another kind of consideration borrowed once more from our societies. In vain have theorists attempted to explain this symmetry by considerations of functional utility. We may prove as much as we like, with Spencer, that locomotion demanded that organisms pass from radial symmetry to bilateral symmetry, which is lesser but more perfect, and that where the maintenance of symmetry was incompatible with the health of the individual or the perpetuation of the species (for example in flatfish), the symmetry has been broken, in an exception to the general rule. But it should not be forgotten that wherever possible, all that could be retained of the primordial symmetry whence life originated (probably spherical, that is to say full and vague), and all that could be derived from the precise and truly beautiful symmetry at which life arrives in its progress, has been conserved or realized. Through the whole gamut of plant and animal life, from diatoms to orchids, from corals to man, the tendency towards symmetry is evident. Where does this tendency come from? Observe that, in our social world, everything which results not from a competition of intermingled plans which clash together, but from an individual's design executed without hindrance, is symmetrical and regular. Kant's philosophical monument where volumes and chapters harmoniously reflect one another; the administrative, financial and military systems established by Napoleon I; the cities which the English have built in Guyana, with their streets drawn by ruler, meeting at right angles, ending in a square surrounded by lowered porticos; our churches, our railway stations, and so on; everything, to repeat, which emanates from a thought which is free, ambitious and strong, master of itself and of others, seems to obey some internal necessity in displaying the luxury of striking regularity and symmetry. Every despot has a love of symmetry; if a writer, he must have constant antitheses; if a philosopher, repeated dichotomies and trichotomies; if a king, ceremony, etiquette, and military parades. If so, and if, as will be shown below, the possibility of individuals' executing their plans completely and on a large scale is a sign of social progress, it follows necessarily that the symmetrical and regular nature of living things attests to the high degree of perfection achieved by cellular societies, and to the enlightened despotism to which they are subject. We should not lose sight of the fact that, since cellular societies are a thousand times older than human societies, the inferiority of the latter is hardly surprising. Besides, human societies are limited in their progress by the small number of men which the planet can support. The greatest empire of the world, China, has only 300 or 400 million subjects. An organism which contained only this number of *ultimate* anatomical elements would necessarily be placed towards the bottom of the scale of plant or animal life.

Having thus met the objection which draws on organic form to argue against the similarity of organisms to social groups, it behoves us to say a word about another not inconsequential objection. Some have contrasted the variability of human societies, even those which are slowest to change, with the relative fixity of organic species. But if, as can be shown, the almost exclusive cause of the internal differentiation of a social form should be sought in the extra-social relations of its members, that is, in their relations, either with the fauna, the flora, the soil, the atmosphere of their country, or with the members of foreign societies which are differently constituted, this difference is not surprising. Due to the very nature of its arrangement—which is entirely *superficial* and not *voluminous*, almost without thickness—to the extreme dispersion of its elements, and to the multiplicity of intellectual and industrial exchanges between one people and another, the social aggregate of men includes an unusually low proportion of essentially conservative intra-social relations between its members, and prevents them from maintaining among themselves the *omnilateral* social relations presupposed by the globular form of a cell or an organism.

In support of the above view, we may remark that external cutaneous cells, which have a monopoly on the principal extra-social relations, are in every case the most easily modifiable. Nothing is more *variable* than the skin and its appendages; in plants, the epidermis is in different cases glabrous, hairy, spiny, etc. This cannot be explained solely by the heterogeneity of the external environment, which is presumed to be greater than that of the internal environment. This latter point is not at all proven. Besides, and consequently, it is always the external cells which set in motion the variations of the rest of the organism. The proof is that the internal organs of new species, although modified to some extent relative to the species from which they emerge, always undergo a lesser modification than do the peripheral organs, and seem to be laggards on the path of organic progress.[37]

Is it necessary to point out that, in the same way, most revolutions in a State are due to the internal fermentation produced by the introduction of new ideas which mobile populations, sailors,

37. To cite only one example, M C Vogt says (in 1879, at a congress of Swiss naturalists, speaking of *Archaeopteryx macroura*, intermediate between reptiles and birds): 'I believe I have proved that adaptation to flight [in reptiles in the process of becoming birds] works from the outside to the inside, from the skin to the skeleton, and that the latter can remain perfectly intact ... while the skin has already come to develop feathers'.

soldiers returned from campaigns in distant parts such as the Crusades, bring back every day from foreign lands? One would hardly be mistaken in seeing an organism as a jealous and closed city, just as the ancients dreamed.

I will pass over a number of secondary objections which the application of the sociological point of view may encounter along its way. Since, after all, the fundamental nature of things is strictly inaccessible, and we are obliged to construct hypotheses in order to penetrate it, let us openly adopt this one and push it to its conclusion. *Hypotheses fingo*, I say naively. What is dangerous in the sciences are not tightly linked conjectures, logically followed to the ultimate depths or the ultimate precipices, but rather the ghosts of ideas which float aimlessly in the mind. The universal sociological point of view seems to me to be one of these spectres which haunt the brains of our speculative contemporaries. Let us from the start see where it will lead us. Let us push ideas to their extreme, at the risk of being taken for extravagant. In this matter in particular, the fear of ridicule is the most antiphilosophical of sentiments. All the developments which follow will be aimed at demonstrating the profound renewal which the sociological interpretation must, or should, bring about in every domain of knowledge.

As a preamble, let us take an example at random. From our point of view, what is signified by the great truth that every activity of the soul is linked to the functioning of some bodily apparatus? It comes down to the fact that in a society no individual can act socially, or show himself in any respect, without the collaboration of a great number of other individuals, most of them unknown to him. The obscure labourers who, by the accumulation of tiny facts, prepare the appearance of a great scientific theory formulated by a Newton, a Cuvier, or a Darwin, compose in some sense the organism of which this genius is the soul; and their labours are the cerebral vibrations of which this theory is the consciousness. Consciousness means in some sense the *cerebral glory* of the brain's most influential and powerful element. Thus, left to its own devices, a monad can achieve nothing. This is the crucial fact, and it immediately explains another, *the tendency of monads to assemble*. This tendency expresses, I believe, the need for a maximum of expended belief. When this maximum is attained at the point of universal cohesion, then desire, now entirely fulfilled, will be annihilated, and time will come to an end. Let us also observe that the obscure labourers I mentioned above may sometimes have as much merit, erudition, and force of thought, as the celebrated beneficiary of their labours, or indeed even more. I make this remark in passing, to address the prejudice which leads us to judge all external monads inferior to ourselves. If the ego is only a director monad among the myriads of commensal monads in the same skull, why, fundamentally, should we believe the latter to be inferior? Is a monarch necessarily more intelligent than his ministers or his subjects?

V

This may all seem very strange, but, fundamentally, it is much less strange than the view which hitherto has been commonly accepted among scientists and philosophers, and from which the universal sociological point of view should logically deliver us. It is truly surprising to see men of science, so stubborn in repeating at every turn that *nothing is created*, admit implicitly as though self-evident that *relations between distinct beings can of themselves become new beings numerically added to the former*. Nonetheless, this is admitted, perhaps unsuspectingly, whenever, having set aside the monadic hypothesis, one tries by means of any other hypothesis, and in particular by the play of atoms, to account for the advent of two crucial beings, namely that of a new living individual, and that of a new ego. Unless we refuse the name of being to these two realities which are the prototypes of any concept of being, we are forced to admit that, as soon as a determinate number of mechanical elements enter into a certain kind of mechanical relation, a new living thing which previously did not exist suddenly exists and is added to their number; more strictly, we should admit that, as soon as a given number of living elements find themselves drawn together in the desired fashion within a skull, something as real as, if not more real than these elements is created in their midst, simply in virtue of this drawing together, as if a number could be increased by the disposition and rearrangement of its units. The ordinary concept of the relation of conditions to outcome, which is so much abused by the natural and social sciences, conceals this almost mythological absurdity which I have described, but nonetheless still harbours it at its very root. Once embarked on this course, there is no reason to stop: every harmonious, profound and intimate *relation* between natural elements becomes the *creator* of a new and superior element, which in turn assists in the creation of another yet higher element; at every step of the scale of phenomenal complexity, from the atom to the ego, *via* a series of increasingly complex molecules, then the cell or the Haeckelian plastidule,[38] then the organ and finally the organism, there will appear as many newly created beings as newly apparent unities and, up to the ego, one will proceed invincibly on the path of this error and encounter no obstacle, since it is impossible for us to know intimately the true nature of the elementary relations which arise in systems of external elements of which we do not form a part. But a serious pitfall appears when we arrive at human societies; here we are at home, we are the true elements of these coherent systems of persons which we call cities or states, regiments or congregations. We know everything that goes on in them. Now, however intimate, profound, and harmonious a given social group may be, we will never see springing forth *ex abrupto* from among its members, to their surprise, a *collective ego* which is real and not only metaphorical, a marvellous outcome of which these individuals would be the conditions. Doubtless there is always one member who represents and personifies the whole group, or else a small number of them (like the ministers of a State) who, each in a different respect, individualize it no less entirely in themselves. But this leader or leaders are always also members of the group, born from their father and mother and not collectively from their subjects or their subordinates. Why, then, should the agreement of unconscious brain cells have the gift of daily awakening from nothingness a consciousness in an embryonic brain, when the agreement of human consciousnesses could never achieve this in a society?

VI

Thus the extension of this most eminently lucid of points of view, namely the sociological, to the totality of phenomena is destined to radically transform the scientific concept of the relation of conditions to result. In still another respect it brings about a profound change in this relation. The principal objection against the monadic doctrine, as stated above, is that it introduces, or appears to introduce, as much complexity at the base of the phenomena as at their summit. What, we will be asked, explains the spiritual complexity of the agents by which we hope to explain all else? I have already met this objection by denying the hypothesized complexity, if it is to be supposed that belief and desire are all there is

---

38. [Trans. Note: The plastidule, in Haeckel's theory, is the basic molecule of protoplasm from which cellular organisms are built up.]

to the monads. However, it may be posited, in my view correctly, that their content cannot be reduced to these two quantities alone. I shall shortly state what more I attribute to them. Returning to the stated objection, then, I shall attack it at its very source, in the widespread prejudice according to which the result is always more complex than its conditions, and the action more differentiated than its agents, whence it follows that universal evolution is necessarily a movement from the homogenous to the heterogeneous, in a progressive and constant process of differentiation. Spencer has the merit, in particular in his chapter on the instability of the homogenous,[39] of having magisterially formulated this belief, and elevated it to the status of law. The truth is that difference comes about by differing and that change comes about by changing and, in thus being given as ends to themselves, change and difference attest to their necessary and absolute character; but it is not and cannot be proven that the total amount of difference and change in the world is either growing or diminishing. If we look at the social world, the only one known to us *from the inside*, we see agents, men, much more differentiated and more sharply characterized as individuals, and richer in continual variations, than are the mechanisms of government or the systems of laws or of beliefs, or even dictionaries or grammars, and this differentiation is maintained by their competition. A historical fact is simpler and clearer than the states of mind of any of its actors. Moreover, as the population of social groups grows and the brains of their members are enriched with new ideas and new sentiments, the functioning of their administrations, their codes of law and conduct, their catechisms, and the very structure of their languages become simpler and more regular, rather as scientific theories become simpler as they are filled with more numerous and diverse facts. Our railway stations are constructed to a simpler and more standardized form than the castles of the Middle Ages, even though the former draw on a much more diverse range of resources and skills. At the same time we see that, if the progress of civilization in certain respects diversifies individual human beings, it does so only on condition of levelling them in other respects by the growing uniformity of their laws, their habits, their customs, and their languages. In general, the similarity of these collective factors encourages the intellectual and moral dissimilarity of individuals, and extends

---

39. [Trans. Note: Herbert Spencer, *First Principles*, 5th ed., London, Williams & Norgate, 1887, ch. 13, pp. 401-430.]

their sphere of action; and besides, if in the course of the civilizing movement, institutions, customs, clothing, industrial products and so on, differ much less *between one point and another* in a given territory, they differ much more *from one moment to another* in a given span of time.

As for the formula of *the instability of the homogenous*, it presupposes that the more homogenous something is, the more unstable its internal equilibrium, to the extent that if it were absolutely homogenous, it would be unable to subsist from one moment to the next. However, it is remarkable that space is the only type of absolute homogeneity known to us, if its reality be admitted, *as Spencer does*. How can it be, if this law holds, that this perfectly homogenous system of points and volumes has subsisted unalterably since the beginning of time? To be sure, this argument no longer holds if the reality of space be denied, but regardless, this putative law is contradicted by a thousand examples of relative homogeneity arising from heterogeneity, the most striking of which are furnished by the observation of either human or animal societies. The aggregation of polyps, animals which are often very complicated, forms a colony or polypary, an extremely rudimentary form of aquatic vegetable. The aggregation of men in tribes or nations gives birth to a language, an inferior species of plant whose historical *vegetation*,[40] *growth* and *flourishing*, to use their own expressions, are studied by philosophers.

This, to repeat, is why the infusion of a sociological spirit into the sciences would be eminently conducive to curing them of this prejudice against which I have taken arms. It would then be clear how we should understand this great and beautiful principle of differentiation, which Spencer extended so successfully without, however, being able to reconcile it, as I believe we must, with the no less certain principle of universal co-ordination. The primordial nebula[41] appears to us shrouded in the mists of time, and it is perhaps due only to this distance that it displays to us the homogeneity which forms the point of departure for all cosmogonic theories. Do we have the least knowledge of what antecedent diversities were sacrificed by the condensation of the elements into similar atoms, of the atoms into molecules and celestial spheres,

---

40. [Trans. Note: The use of the term 'vegetation' (*végétation*) to mean growth or development in general is less common now than in Tarde's time in both English and French.]

41. [Trans. Note: The cloud from which the solar system coalesced.]

of molecules into cells and so on, for the benefit of the diversities which came after them (and which were admittedly greater than the former, which is not to say that the one grew from the other)? We know a little better, but still do not fully understand, what it cost to a people of free and wandering savages to agglomerate themselves into bands, and to bands to settle in cities, circling about a pivot of fixed institutions. But when, before our eyes, the provincial diversity of customs, of costumes, of ideas, of accents, and of physical forms, is being levelled by modernity, by the unity of weights and measures, of language, of accent, and even of conversation—a levelling which is the necessary condition for all these minds to come into contact with one another, that is, to begin to work, and to develop more freely their individual characteristics—then the tears of poets and of artists attest to the price of the social picturesqueness which has been sacrificed for the sake of these advantages. Are the newly created differences more considerable than the old ones, in virtue of being more advantageous because they respond to a greater number of desires? No. We have an unfortunate and inexplicable tendency to imagine everything unknown to us as homogenous. Since the former geological states of the planet are much less well known to us than its current state, we think it certain that they were less differentiated, a prejudice against which Lyell frequently protests.[42] Before the telescope which revealed to us the multiformity of nebulae, of stellar forms, double and variable stars, was the universal dream not of immutable and incorruptible heavens beyond those known to us?[43] And in the realm of the infinitely small, which, much more than the infinitely large, has remained inaccessible to our observations, does one not still dream of the philosopher's stone in a thousand forms, the identical atoms of the chemists, or the so-called homogenous protoplasm of the naturalists? But everywhere where a scientist digs beneath the indistinction which is apparent to us, he discovers an unexpected treasury of distinctions. It was once thought that animalcula were homogenous. Ehrenberg[44] examined them

---

42. [Trans. Note: Charles Lyell (1797-1875), geologist. Lyell's 'uniformitarianism' emphasized the identity of the basic geological laws and processes from the distant past to the present.]

43. [Trans. Note: Tarde presumably has in mind Aristotelian cosmology, in which the heavens beyond the moon are made of a fifth element (aether), which is not found in the sublunary world, and which unlike the four earthly elements, does not admit of any change other than local motion.]

44. [Trans. Note: Christian Gottfried Ehrenberg (1795-1876), naturalist.]

through the microscope, and from then on, as Perrier says, 'the soul of everything he did was the belief in the equal complexity of all animals', from infusoria to man. Since solids and liquids are more accessible to our senses than are gases, and the latter more accessible than is ethereal nature, we think that solids or liquids are more different from each other than are gases, and in physics we speak of *ether* and not of *ethers* (although Laplace uses this plural) as we would speak only of *gas* and not of *gases*, if the latter were known to us only by their physical effects—which are remarkably similar—to the exclusion of their chemical properties. When water vapour crystallizes into a thousand different needles or simply liquefies into flowing water, does this condensation really, as we are inclined to think, entail an increase in the differences inherent in the water molecules? No; let us not forget the freedom which the latter formerly enjoyed in the state of gaseous dispersion, their movement in every direction, their impacts, and their infinitely varied distances. Is it then that the differences have decreased? Again, no: all that has happened is that one kind of difference has been substituted for another, that is, internal differences for mutually external ones.

To exist is to differ; difference is, in a sense, the truly substantial side of things; it is at once their ownmost possession and that which they hold most in common. This must be our starting point, and we must refrain from further explaining this principle, since all things come back to it—including identity, which is more usually, but mistakenly, taken as the point of departure. For identity is only the *minimal degree* of difference and hence a kind of difference, and an infinitely rare kind, as rest is only a special case of movement, and the circle only a particular variety of ellipse. To begin from the primordial identity is to posit at the origin of things a prodigiously improbable singularity, an impossible coincidence of multiple beings, at once distinct from and similar to one another; or else the inexplicable mystery of a single simple being, which would subsequently, for no comprehensible reason, suffer division. It is to commit a similar error to that of the ancient astronomers who, in their chimerical explanations of the solar system, began with the circle and not with the ellipse, on the basis that the former is more perfect. Difference is the alpha and omega of the universe; everything begins with difference, with the elements whose innate diversity (which various reasons make probable) can in my view be the only justification of their multiplicity;

everything ends with difference, where, in the higher phenomena of thought and history, it finally breaks free of the narrow circles in which it had bound itself, namely the atomic vortex and the vital vortex, and transforming the very obstacle it faced into a fulcrum, surpasses and transfigures itself. It seems to me that all similarities and all phenomenal repetitions are only intermediaries, which will inevitably be found to be interposed between some elementary diversities which are more or less obliterated, and the transcendent diversities produced by their partial immolation.

We might also observe that every sufficiently prolonged process of evolution exhibits a succession and interlacing of phenomenal layers which are remarkable alternately for the regularity and the caprice, the permanence and the fugacity, of the relations they present to us. The example of society is eminently well-suited to promote an awareness of this central fact, and at the same time to indicate its true significance, by showing that in this series where identity and difference, the indistinct and the well-characterized each reciprocally make use of the other over and over again, the initial and final term is always difference, the characteristic, the bizarre and inexplicable agitation at the basis of all things, which reappears more clearly and sharply after each successive effacement. The speech of men, each with a different accent, intonation, and timbre of voice and gesture: this veritable chaos of discordant heterogeneities is the social element. But at length, general habits of language emerge from this confused Babel, and are formulated as grammatical laws. In their turn the latter serve, by bringing into relation a greater number of speakers, only to throw into relief the particular individual turn taken by their ideas: another kind of discord. And they succeed all the more in the diversification of minds to the extent that they are themselves more fixed and uniform. Take poets, for example. When a language is newly born, they take hold of it and bend it to their disordered fantasy. However, after a certain period of babbling, rhythms and prosodic laws are formulated and imposed; and this takes place in all poetries, be they Hindu, Greek or French. Uniformity appears anew. What purpose does it serve? To better unfold the poets' imaginative resources and to add lustre to each one's individual hue. In proportion to the growing regularity of the rhythmical beating, as it were, of the wings of poetry, its flight paradoxically becomes more capricious. Victor Hugo's prosody with its subtle rules is at once more complex and more rigorous than Racine's. We could equally well have considered scientists rather than poets, and the observation would have led to the same results. Each scientist works apart from the others, although he utilizes their work, thanks to their common language; he puts his temperament, his soul, into the research he undertakes; all is defined, all is individual.

If we could gather in a single place all the researchers who are collectively constructing a science at an early stage of its development (organic chemistry, for example, meteorology, or linguistics), there could be no more bizarre pandemonium than this scientific furnace. And yet in this furnace an impersonal monument is forged,[45] an edifice in glacial grey, where the least trace of the multicoloured psychological states which built it seems to have been absolutely erased. But let us pause for a moment. Science itself is certainly not the last word in progress. Let us imagine it finished, complete, and condensed into a definitive catechism which could easily be installed in a corner of everyone's memory; in this way a vastly greater quantity of energy than we can presently imagine would be made available in the human brain for other uses. It would then become clear that the perfect systematization and universal propagation of scientific orthodoxy had had for its ultimate and supreme rationale the extraordinary flourishing of hypotheses, of philosophical heresies, of an endless series of self-invented systems, and of extraordinary lyrical and dramatic fantasies, in which, thanks to the impersonality of scientific knowledge, each mind's profound need to universalize its particular nuance and to set its seal upon the world could be fully satisfied. Intelligence followed to its logical conclusion will in the end be nothing more than the handmaiden of imagination.

Shall we consider social evolution in its economic, administrative, or military aspect? We will again observe the same law. Industry, from a primitive phase where each does whatsoever and howsoever he likes, evolves rapidly to a second phase where professions and corporations are established, with their fixed and traditional processes of manufacture which seem created to stifle genius, which would be nothing but a useless encumbrance; but on the contrary, by this very constraint, the genius of inventions and of arts is fortified and emerges incomparably more fecund than before. Commerce, from a primitive phase with no fixed or general prices, requiring perpetual haggling, and favouring individual

---

45. [Trans. Note: Reading *se forge* with the 1893 text; the 1895 text has *se forme* (takes shape).]

shrewdness and cunning, evolves to produce the uniform and regulated course of our great modern markets, provided with their special thermometers known as stock exchanges; and in the end, far from crushing individual skill beneath the authority of number, the regularity and almost physical inevitability of the overall economic facts support the unbridled impulse to speculation and the spirit of enterprise which take hold of these facts and play upon them, and in which the least psychological particularities of the players break forth lawlessly in sudden triumphs or catastrophes. The incoherence and administrative quirks of a nation in its embryonic state are gradually replaced by unity, stable administration and centralized power, all to the greater glory of statesmen, who are the operators of this machine and make use of it to accomplish their historic deeds, each one *sui generis* like its author, a marvellous accident of planetary forces. Finally, the indisciplined hordes of barbarian societies are superseded by our fine mechanized armies, in which the individual is nothing but a tool in the hands of a great captain who throws him into some battle dissimilar to every other, with its own name and date, reproducing on the vastly enlarged scale of the battlefield the particular psychological state which is his during the action.

It can thus be seen from these examples that, strangely enough, order and simplicity are manifest in the composite even though foreign to its elements, and then once more disappear in the higher composites, and so on up the scale. But in the case of social evolutions and social aggregations, of which we form a part and where we have the advantage of being able to grasp at the same time the two ends of the chain, the lowest and the highest stones of the edifice, we can clearly see that order and simplicity are simply mediating terms, alembics in which elementary diversity is potently transfigured and, as it were, sublimated. The poet and the philosopher essentially, and secondarily the inventor, the artist, the speculator, the politician, and the tactician: these are the terminal flowers of any national tree;[46] their blossoming depends upon the work of all the aborted germs of innate, extra-social (or in some cases anti-social) characteristics, which every

---

46. I do not at all mean to place all of these on the same level. Among other differences, one may harbour hopes or dreams of a life of perfected civilization, when everyone would have his own poetry and his own philosophy, but one cannot imagine a life where everyone had his own great discovery, his own grand prize in the lottery, or his own political or military role.

private citizen brought with him into the world, and which in most cases were stifled in the cradle by education, that indispensable but false leveller.

These innate characteristics, the first term of the social series, are at the same time the last term of the vital series. In attempting to reascend the latter in its turn, we would traverse first of all the specific form, harmoniously constituted and regularly repeated over centuries, whose variations these characteristics are,—then the critical period in which this form was shaped by a coincidence of multiple causes in unexpected juxtapositions,—then the previous forms whence the specific form derives and their analogous formations,—then the cell, and finally the formless or protean protoplasm, with its sudden whims which no law may grasp.—Here again the alpha and the omega is diversity, in all its vividness.

But is the protoplasm, the first term of the vital series, not also the final term of the chemical series? The latter, if we reascend it in its turn, displays the less and less complex molecular forms of organic chemistry, and the similarly less and less complex molecular forms of inorganic chemistry, all regularly constructed and probably consisting of harmonious cycles of periodic rhythmical movements, but each separated from the others by tumultuous and disordered crises of their combinations; and thus we arrive by conjecture at the simplest atom or atoms, from which all the others are built. But is this, then, the initial element? No. For the simplest atom is a material form, a vortex, as we are told, a vibratory rhythm of a certain kind, something by all appearances infinitely complex. This complexity has been confirmed more than ever by the studies of highly rarefied gases conducted since the invention of the radiometer, in which it seems to be possible to see the gaseous atom individually. For example, in this ultra-gaseous world, a ray of light does not always travel in a straight line;[47] the closer we approach to the individual element, the more variable the observed phenomena. Clerk Maxwell has established that the molecules in the same gas move with very different speeds, even

---

47. [Trans. Note: For this finding, see W. Crookes (1879) 'On the illumination of lines of molecular pressure, and the trajectory of molecules', *Philosophical Transactions of the Royal Society of London*, no. 175, pp.135-164. The 'ultra-gaseous' or 'radiant matter' state refers to matter in an extreme state of rarefaction, where each molecule is 'allowed to obey its own motions or laws without interference', and can be seen as an individual rather than part of an 'aggregate' (W. Crookes (1880) 'On a fourth state of matter', *Proceedings of the Royal Society of London*, no. 30, pp. 469-472. William Crookes (1832-1919), chemist and physicist.]

though their average speed may be identical.[48] Spottiswoode, of the Royal Society of London, says: 'This is because the simplicity of nature as we currently understand it is in reality the result of an infinite complexity, and because, *beneath the appearance of uniformity, we find a diversity whose depths and secrets we have not begun to fathom*'.[49] Crookes expresses himself similarly with relation to radiant matter: 'The greatest problems of the future will find their solution in this unexplored domain [of the infinitely small], where doubtless *the fundamental, subtle, marvellous and profound realities* are to be found'.[50] Would he so express himself if he regarded the ultimate elements, in the vulgar fashion, as identical exemplars of an unvarying form? Because every chemical substance translates itself to our eyes by a special vibration imprinted on the ether, one is led to believe that this faculty of vibrating in a certain way is identical in every similar atom and that they have no other properties. It is as if one said of a grove of pines or poplars, heard at a distance and recognized by its particular whisper or murmur, simple and monotonous, that the leaves of the pine or the poplar consist of a characteristic and invariable quivering. Thus, as with society, as with life, chemistry appears to bear witness to the necessity of universal difference, the principle and end of all hierarchies and all developments.

Diversity, and not unity, is at the heart of things: this conclusion, in any case, follows for us from a general remark which a simple glance at the world and at the sciences allows us to make. Everywhere an exuberant richness of unheard-of variations and modulations springs forth from these permanent themes which are called living species and stellar systems, and from equilibria of all kinds, and in the end destroys and renews them utterly, and yet in no case do the forces or laws which we are used to calling principles have variety as a term or as their goal. Forces, we are told, exist to serve laws, and all laws apply to phenomena to the extent that the latter are perfect repetitions and not repetitions with variations; all laws manifestly tend to ensure the exact reproduction of the themes and the indefinitely prolonged stability of all kinds of equilibria, and to prevent their alteration or renewal. The great crankshaft of our solar system is made *in order to* turn eternally.

---

48. [Trans. Note: James Clerk Marxwell (1831-1879), physicist. The reference is to his statistical description of gas kinetics (the Maxwell-Boltzmann distribution).]
49. [Trans. Note: The citation has not been traced.]
50. [Trans. Note: W. Crookes, the citation has not been traced.]

The doubts which might have persisted on this point after Laplace were dispelled by Le Verrier.[51] Every living species *wants to* perpetuate itself endlessly; something in it struggles to maintain its existence against everything which endeavours to dissolve it. In this respect it is like a government, or like the most precarious ministry whose essential role is always to proclaim, believe and wish that it is installed in power for all eternity. There is no long-extinct plant or animal species, now extant only as a fossil, which did not once embody a *legislative* assurance, an apparently well-founded certainty of living as long as the Earth. All these things which have passed away were once called to endless life, supported by physical, chemical, and vital laws, as our despots and our ministers by their code of laws and by their army. Our solar system too will doubtless perish, like so many others whose wreckage is visible in the skies; and indeed, who knows if the molecular forms themselves will not disappear, having come into existence in the course of the ages at the expense of those which preceded them?

But how can all of this have died, or how could it die? How, if there is in the universe nothing but supposedly immutable and all-powerful laws aiming at stable equilibria, and a supposedly immutable substance to which these laws apply, how could the action of these laws on this substance produce this magnificent flourishing of varieties which rejuvenates the universe at every moment, and this series of unexpected revolutions which transfigure it? How could the least ornament creep into these austere rhythms and enliven even a little the eternal psalmody of the world? From the marriage of the monotonous and the homogenous what could be born but tedium? If everything comes from identity, aims at identity and returns to identity, what is the source of this dazzling torrent of variety? We may be certain that the fundamental nature of things is not as poor, as drab, or as colourless as has been supposed. Forms are only brakes and laws are only dykes erected in vain against the overflowing of revolutionary differences and civil dissensions, in which the laws and forms of tomorrow secretly take shape, and which, in spite of the yokes upon yokes they bear, in spite of chemical and vital discipline, in spite of reason, in spite

---

51. [Trans. Note: Pierre-Simon Laplace (1749-1827, mathematician and astronomer) was instrumental in developing a mechanical theory of the stability of the solar system. Urbain Le Verrier's (1811-1877) prediction of the planet Neptune (1846) and its subsequent discovery by observation provided further confirmation of Laplace's model.]

of celestial mechanics, will one distant day, like the people of a nation, sweep away all barriers and from their very wreckage construct the instrument of a still higher diversity.

Let us insist on this central truth: we may approach it by remarking that, in all great regular mechanisms—the social mechanism, the vital mechanism, the stellar mechanism, or the molecular mechanism—all the internal revolts which in the end break them apart are provoked by a similar condition: their constitutive elements, the soldiers of these diverse regiments, the temporary incarnation of their laws, always belong only by one aspect of their being to the world they constitute, and by other aspects escape it. This world would not exist without them; without the world, conversely, the elements would still be something. The attributes which each element possesses in virtue of its incorporation into its regiment do not form the whole of its nature; it has other tendencies and other instincts which come to it from its other regimentations; and, moreover (we will shortly see the necessity of this corollary), still others which come to it from its basic nature, from itself, from its own fundamental substance which is the basis of its struggle against the collective power of which it forms a part. This collective is wider but no less deep than the element, but it is a merely artificial being, a composite made up of aspects and façades of other beings.—This hypothesis can easily be verified in the case of social elements. If they were only social, and in particular only national, it would follow that societies and nations would exist without change for all eternity. But, in spite of our great debt to the social and national environment, it is clear that we do not owe everything to it. At the same time as being French or English, we are mammals, and as such there circulate in our blood not only the germs of social instincts which predispose us to imitate our peers, to believe what they believe and want what they want, but also the seeds of non-social instincts, including some which are anti-social. Surely, if society had made us in our entirety, it would have made us entirely sociable. It is therefore from the depths of organic life (and from deeper still, we believe) that there wells up among our cities this magma of discord, hatred and envy, which on occasion submerges them. It is hardly possible to enumerate all the States overthrown by sexual love, all the cults it has undermined or denatured, all the languages it has corrupted, and also all the colonies it has founded, all the religions it has ameliorated and made gentle, all the barbaric idioms it has civilized, all the arts whose life-blood it has been! Rebellion and rejuvenation indeed spring from a single source. In truth, all that is truly social is the *imitation* of one's compatriots and ancestors,[52] in the broadest sense of the term.

If the elements of societies are vital in nature, the organic elements of living bodies are chemical. One of the errors of the older physiology was to think that as soon as they enter into an organism, chemical substances abdicate all their properties and are penetrated to their innermost heart, to their most secret core, by the mysterious influence of life. Our contemporary physiologists have entirely dispelled this error. A molecule which forms part of an organic body, therefore, belongs at once to two worlds which are foreign or hostile to one another. Can it be denied that this independence of the chemical nature of corporeal elements with respect to their organic nature helps to explain the perturbations, the deviations and the fortunate recastings of living forms? Indeed, it seems to me that we must go yet further and recognize that only this independence can account for the resistance of some parts of the organs to the acceptance of the inherited living form, and for the necessity which sometimes obliges life (that is, the collection of molecules which have remained obedient) to finally come to a compromise with the rebellious faction of molecules by adopting a new form. In effect, then, the only truly vital process seems to be *generation* (of which nutrition and cellular regeneration are only special cases), in conformity with the hereditary form.

Is this the final word? Perhaps not; the analogy suggests that chemical and astronomical laws themselves are not supported on nothingness, but that their domain of application is populated by tiny beings already endowed with inner characters and innate diversities, diversities which are in no way accommodated to the particularities of the celestial or chemical machinery. It is true that we cannot perceive in chemical bodies the trace of any accidental ailment or deviation which we could see as parallel to organic disorders or social revolutions. But, since there do currently exist chemical heterogeneities, there doubtless existed, in some far distant era, chemical formations. Were these formations simultaneous? Did hydrogen, carbon, nitrogen, etc., appear at the same instant in the heart of a single amorphous substance which was previously

---

52. In progressive societies, it is increasingly one's compatriots rather than one's ancestors who are imitated, and the converse in stationary societies. But to associate always and everywhere means to assimilate, that is, to imitate.

non-chemical? If this is judged improbable, or rather impossible, we must admit that an originary atomic form transmitted through vibration, starting from a point—that of hydrogen, for example—imposed itself throughout the whole or almost the whole of material extension, and that, by breaking away in succession from the primordial hydrogen, at long intervals of time, all the other so-called simple bodies—whose atomic weights, as we know, are often exact multiples of that of hydrogen—were formed. But how can we explain such fission on the hypothesis that the primitive elements are perfectly homogenous and governed by the same law, which, it seems to me, should rather consolidate by the identity of their structure the identity and immutability of their nature? Will it perhaps be argued that the accidents of astronomical evolution involving the primitive elements could have produced or catalysed chemical formations? Unfortunately this hypothesis seems to me to have been very clearly ruled out by the discovery of the spectroscope. Since, according to this instrument, all the so-called simple bodies or many of them enter into the composition of the most distant planets and stars, which have evolved independently of each other, common sense tells us that the simple bodies were formed before the stars, as cloth before clothes. It follows that the piecemeal dismembering of the primitive substance admits of only one explanation: namely, that the particles were originally dissimilar, and that their schisms were caused by this essential dissimilarity. There is thus some reason to think that hydrogen, for example, as it exists today after so many successive eliminations or emigrations, is noticeably different from the ur-hydrogen, which would have been a pell-mell of discordant atoms. The same observation applies to all the simple bodies which were subsequently engendered. In being thus exhausted and reduced, each was consolidated in its equilibrium, and fortified by its very losses. But, if so, it is highly improbable, despite the extraordinary stability thus acquired by the oldest atomic or molecular forms, that complete similarity obtains among the elements which subsist in each. It would have sufficed, for the refining of each form to come to an end, if the internal differences of its elements had diminished to a point where it was no longer impossible for the elements to coexist. These infinitesimal citizens of mysterious cities are so distant from us[53] that it is no wonder that the noise of their internal dis-

---

53. I say distant from us, not only by the incommensurable distance between their smallness and our relative immensity, and, conversely, between their relative

cord does not reach us, and their internal differences, if they exist as I believe, must be of a fineness which cannot be apprehended by our gross instruments. However, the polymorphism of certain elements is a sufficient indicator that they harbour dissidences, and we know enough of these to have some suspicion of the troubles and disparities which afflict the fundamental nature of the principal substances employed by life, in particular carbon. How can it be admitted that the atoms of a single substance bond with each other so as to form what Gerhardt calls hydrogen hydride, chlorine chloride, etc., while persisting in elevating to the status of dogma the perfect similarity of the multiple atoms of a single substance? Does not such a union presuppose a difference of at least an equal magnitude to the sexual difference which allows two individuals of a single species to unite intimately, and without which they could only bump together?

If we observe that the element in which these unions of atom to similar atom have been most clearly demonstrated to be probable, and indeed almost certain, namely carbon, is also the element which manifests itself to us in its pure state in the most varied aspects, diamond, graphite, coal, etc., the preceding induction will be confirmed. It is no surprise that the body most fertile in varieties reveals most clearly the vigorous marriages between its constituent atoms ... Carbon is the differentiated element *par excellence*.

Wurtz says: 'The affinity of carbon for carbon is the cause of the infinite variety and the immense number of the combinations of carbon; it is the *raison d'être* of organic chemistry. No other element possesses to the same degree this master-property of carbon, this faculty which its atoms have of combining with one another, of fastening onto one another, of forming this framework, so variable in its form, its dimensions, its solidity, and which serves, as it were, as the basis of other materials'.[54]

After carbon, the bodies which have to the greatest degree this capacity for being partially or entirely saturated by themselves are oxygen, hydrogen and nitrogen; remarkably enough, exactly those substances utilized by life!

Besides, one significant fact should give us pause for reflection: life began on this globe at a particular time and in a particular

---

apparent eternity and our brief duration (a very strange and perhaps imaginary contrast), but also by the profound heterogeneity of their inner nature and ours.

54. [Trans. Note: Adolphe Wurtz (1817-1884), chemist. The citation has not been traced.]

place. Why at this place and not elsewhere, if the same substances were composed of the same elements? Let us even admit that life is only a particular, highly complex chemical combination. Nonetheless, how could it have been born, if not from an element unlike all the others?

VII

In the two preceding chapters, we have shown that the universal sociological point of view may be of service to science in two ways, by liberating it, first, from those hollow entities brought about by misunderstanding the relation of conditions to result, and then mistakenly substituted for the real agents; and second, from the prejudiced belief in the perfect similarity of these elementary agents. These two advantages are, however, purely negative; I will now try to show what more positive information we can gain by the same method regarding the inner nature of the elements. It is not enough to say that the elements are diverse, we must specify in what their diversity consists. This will demand several developments of our theory.

What is society? It could be defined, from our point of view, as each individual's reciprocal possession, in many highly varied forms, of every other. Unilateral possession, such as that in ancient law of the slave by the master, of the son by the father, or of the wife by the husband, is only a first step towards the social link. Thanks to the development of civilization, the possessed becomes more and more a possessor, and the possessor a possessed, until, by equality of right, by popular sovereignty, and by the equitable exchange of services, ancient slavery, now mutualized and universalized, makes each citizen at once the master and the servant of every other. At the same time, the ways of possessing one's fellow citizens, and of being possessed by them, grow in number every day. Every new administration or industry which is created sets to work new administrators or industrialists on behalf of those who are administered by them or who consume their products, and who in this sense gain a real right with respect to them, a right which they did not previously have, while they themselves conversely have come, by this new two-sided relation, to *belong to* these industrialists or administrators. We may say the same of any new opportunity. When a newly opened railway brings produce from the sea to a small town far inland for the first time, the domain of the town's inhabitants has grown to include the fishermen who are now part of it, and the clientele of the fishermen, correspondingly, has grown to include the townspeople. As a subscriber to a newspaper, I possess *my* journalists, who possess *their* subscribers. I possess my government, my religion, my police force, just as much as my specifically human form, my temperament, and my health; but I also know that the ministers of my nation, the priests of my confession or the police officers of my county count me as one of the flock they guard; and in the same way, the human form, if it were somehow personified, would see in me only one of *its* particular variations.

All philosophy hitherto has been based on the verb *Be*, the definition of which was the philosopher's stone, which all sought to discover. We may affirm that, if it had been based on the verb *Have*, many sterile debates and fruitless intellectual exertions would have been avoided. From this principle, *I am*, all the subtlety in the world has not made it possible to deduce any existence other than my own: hence the negation of external reality. If, however, the postulate *I have* is posited as the fundamental fact, both that which *has* and that which *is had* are given inseparably at once.

If having seems to indicate being, being surely implies having. Being, that hollow abstraction, is never conceived except as the *property* of something, of some other being, which is itself composed of *properties*, and so on to infinity. At root, the whole content of the concept of being is exhausted by the concept of having. But the converse is not true: being is not the whole content of the idea of property.

The concrete and substantial concept which one discovers in oneself is, therefore, that of having. Instead of the famous *cogito ergo sum*, I would prefer to say: *I desire, I believe, therefore I have*. The verb *to be* means in some cases *to have*, and in others *to be equal to*. 'My arm is hot': the heat of my arm is the property of my arm. Here *is* means *has*. 'A Frenchman is a European, a metre is a measure of length'. Here *is* means *is equal to*. But this equality itself is only the relation of part to whole, of genus to species or *vice versa*, that is, a kind of relation of possession. In these two meanings, therefore, *being* is reducible to having.

If one wishes to forcibly draw from the concept of *Being* implications which are precluded by its essential sterility, one has to put it in opposition to non-being, and grant to the latter term (which is nothing but an empty objectification of our faculty of denial, as Being is an objectification of our faculty of affirmation) a wholly unwarranted importance.—In this respect, the Hegelian system can be considered the last word in the philosophy of Being. Embarked on this path, one will have to concoct impenetrable, and basically contradictory, concepts of *becoming* and *disappearance*, the old empty pap of Teutonic ideologues.[55] By contrast, nothing could be clearer than the concepts of *gain* and *loss*, of acquisition and divestment, which take this place in the philosophy of Having, if we may thus name something which does not yet exist. Between being and non-being there is no middle term, whereas one can have more or less.

Being and non-being, ego and non-ego: barren oppositions which obscure the real correlatives. The true opposite of the *ego* is not the non-ego but the *mine*; the true opposite of being, that is of having, is not non-being but *what is had*.

The deep and accelerating divergence between the course of science strictly speaking and that of philosophy comes from the fact that the former, happily, has chosen for its guide the verb Have. For science, everything is explained by *properties*, not by entities. Science disdains the unsatisfactory relation of substance to phenomenon, two empty terms which only are only the doubles of Being; it makes only moderate use of the relation of cause to effect, in which possession appears in only one of its two forms, and the less important, namely possession by desire. But science has made considerable use and, unfortunately, abuse of the relation of *proprietor*[56] to *property*. The abuse has consisted primarily in having misunderstood this relation by failing to see that the real property of any proprietor is a set of other proprietors; that each mass, each molecule of the solar system, for example, has for its physical and mechanical property not words like extension, mobility and so on, but all the other masses, all the other molecules; that each atom of a molecule has for its chemical property, not atomicities or

---

55. [Trans. Note: In Hegel's logic, the 'disappearance' (*Verschwinden*) of being into non-being and *vice versa* generates 'becoming' (*Werden*) (*Science of Logic*, vol 1, book 1, sec 1, ch 1.C.1, 'Unity of Being and Nothing').]

56. [Trans. Note: Tarde's concept of 'property' (*propriété*) is deliberately ambiguous between the sense of 'goods owned' and the sense of 'characteristic' or 'quality'. The term 'proprietor' (*propriétaire*) is standard in both French and English for a person who has a property in the first sense, but not in the second. In English-language analytic philosophy, 'instance' is sometimes used to describe an entity which has a property in the second sense (which 'instantiates' the property), but this brings with it an implicit ontology of properties which is incompatible with Tarde's; I have therefore retained the term 'proprietor'. The theory of properties is discussed further in the Afterword.]

affinities, but all the other atoms of the same molecule; that each cell of an organism has for its biological property, not irritability, contractibility, innervation, and so on, but all the other cells of the same organism, and in particular, of the same organ. Here possession is reciprocal, as in every *intra-social* relation; but it can be unilateral, as in the *extra-social* relation of master to slave, or of the farmer to his cattle. For example, the retina has for its property, not vision, but the luminously vibrating ethereal atoms, which do not possess it; and the mind possesses mentally all the objects of its thought, to which it in no way belongs. Is this to say that the abstract terms, mobility, density, weight, affinity, and so on, express nothing and correspond to nothing? They mean, I think, that beyond the real domain of every element, there is its conditionally necessary domain, that is certain although unreal, and that the ancient distinction between the real and the possible, in a new sense, is not a chimera.

The elements are, certainly, agents as much as they are proprietors; but they can be proprietors without being agents, and they cannot be agents without being proprietors. Moreover, their action can be revealed to us only as a change in the nature of their possession.

On closer investigation, it will be seen that the sole cause of the superiority of the scientific point of view over the philosophical point of view is the fortunate choice of fundamental relation adopted by scientists, and that all the remaining obscurities and weaknesses of science spring from the incomplete analysis of this relation.

For thousands of years, thinkers have catalogued the different ways of being and the different degrees of being, and have never thought to classify the different types and degrees of possession. Possession is, nonetheless, the universal fact, and there is no better term than *acquisition* to express the formation and growth of any being. The terms *correspondence* and *adaptation*,[57] brought into fashion by Darwin and Spencer, are more vague and equivocal, and grasp the universal fact only from the outside. Is it true that the bird's wing is adapted to air, the fish's fin to water, the eye to light? No, no more than the locomotive is adapted to coal, or the

---

57. [Trans. Note. 'Adaptation' refers to Darwin's concept of the process through which a population becomes better suited to its environment through natural selection. Herbert Spencer developed Darwin's idea by seeing adaptation as a process of increasing 'correspondence' between the organism and its environment.]

sewing machine to the seamstress' thread. Shall we also say that the vasomotor nerves, the ingenious mechanism by which the internal equilibrium of the body's temperature is maintained despite variations in the external temperature, are adapted to these variations? *Fighting against* would be a curious form of *adapting to*! The locomotive is adapted, if you will, to terrestrial locomotion, and the wing to aerial locomotion, and this comes down to saying that the wing utilizes the air to move, as the locomotive uses coal, as the fin uses water. Does this using not mean taking possession? Every being wants, not to make itself appropriate *for* external beings, but to appropriate *them* for itself. Atomic or molecular bonding[58] in the physical world, nutrition in the living world, perception in the intellectual world, law in the social world, possession in its innumerable forms never ceases to extend from a being to other beings, by the interlacing of various and increasingly subtle domains.

It is variable in its infinite degrees as well as in its multiple forms. Stars, for example, possess each other with an intensity which grows or shrinks in inverse proportion to the square of their distance. The vitality of organisms, that is the intimate solidarity of their parts, rises or falls continuously. From deepest sleep to the most perfect clarity of mind, thought ranges over a wide gamut which marks the growth of its special dominion over the world. When security is re-established in a country which has been subject to great upheavals, does each citizen not still feel himself to be master of those of his compatriots from whom he has the right to expect some service—that is to say, of all his compatriots—and on whose legitimate help he relies more strongly than before?

Whatever form possession takes, be it physical, chemical, vital, mental, or social (not to speak of the subdivisions of each form), we must first distinguish whether it is unilateral or reciprocal, and second, whether it is established between an element and one or more other elements considered individually, or between an element and an indistinct group of other elements. Let us first speak briefly of this second distinction. When I enter into verbal communication with one or several of my fellows, our respective monads, in my view, reciprocally grasp each other; at least, it is certain that this relation is the relation of a social element with other social elements that are taken as distinct. By contrast, when

---

58. [Trans. Note: Tarde uses the term 'adhesion' (*adhérence*), but appears to have the more general concept of 'bonding' in mind.]

I look at, listen to, or study nature, rocks, water, or even plants, each object of my thought is a hermetically closed world of elements, which all doubtless know each other or grasp each other intimately, like the members of a social group, but which can be encompassed by me only as a whole and from the outside. The chemist can only hypothesize the atom, and is certain of never being able to act on it individually. Matter, as the chemist understands and uses the concept, is a compact dust of distinct atoms, whose distinctions are effaced by their enormous number and by the illusory continuity of their actions. In the living but inanimate, or apparently inanimate, world, can our monad find some less confused phantom, and grasp it? It seems it can. The element, already, intuits the element; the girl who tends a flower loves it with a devotion which no diamond could inspire in her.

We must, however, look to the social world to see monads laid bare, grasping each other in the intimacy of their transitory characters, each fully unfolded before the other, in the other, by the other. This is the relation *par excellence*, the paradigm of possession of which all others are only sketches or reflections. By persuasion, by love and hate, by personal prestige, by common beliefs and desires, or by the mutual chain of contract, in a kind of tightly knit network which extends indefinitely, social elements hold each other or pull each other in a thousand ways, and from their competition the marvels of civilization are born.

Are not the marvels of organization and life born from a similar action, from vital element to vital element, and doubtless from atom to atom? I am inclined to think so, for reasons which it would take too long to explain here. Must it not be likewise for chemical creations and for astronomical formations? Newtonian attraction surely acts from one atom to another, since the most complicated chemical operations do not alter it at all.

In that case, the possessive action of monad upon monad, of element upon element, would be the only truly fertile relation. As for the action of a monad, or at least of an element, on a confused group of indiscriminate monads or elements, or conversely, it would only be an accidental perturbation of the wonderful works wrought by the elements' duel or by their marriage. As much as the relation of element to element is creative, so the relation of element to group is destructive, but both are necessary.

Unilateral possession and reciprocal possession are, likewise, necessarily united. But the latter is superior to the former. It is reciprocal possession which explains the formation of those beautiful celestial mechanisms in which, by the power of mutual attraction, every point is a centre. Reciprocal possession explains the creation of these admirable living organisms whose parts are all united and solidary, and where everything is both an end and a means at once. By reciprocal possession, finally, in the free cities of antiquity and in modern states, mutuality of service and equality of right bring about the prodigious achievements of our sciences, industries, and arts. Let us observe that, if organized beings resulted from a process of fabrication by a single being, or from the regular differentiation of a single homogenous substance, it would be impossible to account for our surprising ability to see the parts of these beings as made for the whole, or the whole as made for the parts. Beings, or rather manufactured objects, would be, with respect to the manufacturer, that which our furniture or tools are to us: mere means, which no sophistical juggling will ever disguise as ends with respect to our acts. As for the unique substance which, some think, creates particular beings by spontaneously splitting itself, it is impossible to see why, first, if it carried no goal within itself, it would have emerged from its primitive undifferentiated state; nor, secondly, why, prior to any differentiation, alone in the world, it took a roundabout way to attain its goal rather than going straight there, used a means instead of grasping its end directly, and preferred the tortuous paths of *evolution* to the short and easy way of immediate *actuation*. Finally, even leaving aside these insurmountable difficulties, it is impossible to answer this question: how, once it decided to evolve, to take this roundabout way to attain its goal or goals, was this unique substance able to will one thing for this and another thing for that, that is, to neutralize each act of will by another, which comes down to having no will at all, and which, to repeat, makes its subsequent differentiation incomprehensible?

By contrast, on the hypothesis of the monads, everything follows naturally. Each monad draws the world to itself, and thus has a better grasp of itself. Of course, they are parts of each other, but they can belong to each other to a greater or lesser extent, and each aspires to the highest degree of possession; whence their gradual concentration; and besides, they can belong to each other in a thousand different ways, and each aspires to learn new ways to appropriate its peers. Hence their transformations. They transform in order to conquer; but, since none will ever submit to another except out of self-interest, none can fully accomplish its ambitious dream, and the sovereign monad is exploited by its vassal monads, even as it makes use of them.

The bizarre and grimacing character of reality, visibly torn apart by fratricidal wars, followed by awkward transactions, demonstrates that the world contains multiple agents. Their multiplicity attests to their diversity, and finds its reason only in this diversity. Already born diverse, the agents tend to diversify themselves even further, as their nature demands; on the other hand, their diversity depends on their being not unities, but totalities of a special form.

It seems to me, moreover, that many perplexing enigmas could be resolved by imagining that the speciality of each element, a true universal medium (*milieu*), is to be not only a totality, but a certain kind of virtuality, and to incarnate within itself a cosmic idea which is always called, but rarely destined, to realize itself effectively. This would be, as it were, to house Plato's ideas in Epicurus' atoms, or rather Empedocles', since, if Zeller is to be believed, the latter apparently professed, like Leibniz, the diversity of elements.[59] It is useful, now and again, to be able to take shelter behind some Greek ancestor.

Two points are evidently lacking in current transformist theories of evolution. In conflict with the force which tends to conserve living forms, they imagine a diversifying force, which they then do not know where to put. In general they disperse it outside the organism, in accidents of climate, of environment, of nutrition, or of growth, and refuse to recognize an internal cause of diversity at the heart of the organism itself. Secondly, whether projected from inside or stimulated from outside, specific variations, which are the building blocks of the Darwinian system, are divergences without an aim, rebellions without a programme, disordered fantasies. However, do we not see, under an established and consistent government, the essential sterility and mutual neutralization of oppositions which are not enflamed by any political ideal of their own, by any dream of social palingenesis? It is impossible to conceive that such madness could triumph in a living being,

---

59. [Trans. Note: Epicurus did hold that atoms were of distinct kinds, but they are not as clearly differentiated as the four elements of Empedocles (earth, air, fire and water). Leibniz held that each monads or element must be qualitatively distinct from every other (*Monadology* §§8-9), and saw this as an argument against atomism of the Epicurean type.]

or that it could be of any possible use; and, were this madness to persist for the maximum astronomically possible duration, this would not be long enough to make remotely probable the fortuitous agreement of these ruptures of equilibrium in a new vital equilibrium, the construction of a new order from this accumulated disorder. But, on our hypothesis, the force of diversification of forms, as much as the force of their conservation, has a tangible support within the organism, and it has a direction. We must see every spontaneous modification of a living species, even the most fleeting, as *aiming* towards another species, which it would attain if exaggerated sufficiently.

Among the variations, let us not confuse those which are produced accidentally and from outside, by the vagaries of chance, and those which are due to the long-standing struggle, in the heart of each organism or of each state, between the triumphant ideal that constitutes it, and the constricted and stifled ideals which chafe beneath its yoke, yearning to emerge and blossom forth. The former are usually neutralized; in most cases it is only the latter which come to fruition. All historians, knowingly or not, make this distinction. Beside the great facts which they relate often, for the sake of their conscience, they emphasize with special care the smallest reforms and the most obscure discussions, barely noted by their contemporaries, which attest to the appearance of new religious or political ideas. For example, the slow encroachment of royal power upon the feudal order, the skirmishes between parliaments and kings, between commoners and lords. Such and such an obscure act of Philip the Fair, which demonstrates a clear orientation towards the still distant administrative centralization of modern France, is of more value to the historian than the trial of the Templars.[60] However bad a social constitution may be, it will last until another is conceived. However false the reigning philosophical system, it will persist until the day when a new theory comes to dethrone it.

VIII

Since being is having (*avoir*), it follows that everything must be avid (*avide*). Now, if there is anything so obvious as to strike

---

60. [Trans. Note: The reign of Philip IV the Fair of France (r. 1285-1314) has been seen by historians as marking a transition from a charismatic to a more bureaucratic, modern form of monarchical rule. He initiated the suppression of the Knights Templar in 1307 and disbanded the Order in 1312.]

everyone's eye, it is surely this avidity, the immense ambition which from end to end of the world, from the vibrating atom or the prolific animalcule to the conquering king, fills and moves every being. Every possibility tends towards its realization, every reality tends towards its universalization. Every possibility tends to realize itself, to characterize itself precisely: whence the overflowing of variations above and across the living themes, both physical and social. Every reality, every characteristic, once formed, tends to universalize itself. This is the reason why light and heat radiate and why electricity propagates with such evident rapidity, and the least atomic vibration aspires by itself to fill the infinite ether, a goal to which every other vibration lays a competing claim. This is why every species, every living race be it barely formed, multiplying in a geometric progression, would soon cover the entire globe, if it did not come up against its equally fertile rivals, and not only species and races, but all minimally distinct particularities, and even their ailments, a fact which rules out any teleological explanation of fertility falsely considered as a means to the preservation of forms. Finally, this is why any social product whatever which has its own more or less well-defined character, an industrial product, a line of verse, a formula, some political idea which appears one day in a corner of someone's brain, dreams like Alexander of the conquest of the world, seeks to project itself in thousands and millions of copies everywhere men live, and stops in this path only when blocked by the force of its no less ambitious rival. The three principal forms of universal repetition, wave-like, generative, imitative, as I have said elsewhere,[61] are so many procedures of government and instruments of conquest which give rise to the three kinds of physical, vital, and social invasion: vibratory radiation, generative expansion, and the contagion of the example.

The child is born a despot: like an African king, as far as he is concerned, the other exists only to serve him. Years of punishment and educational constriction are required to cure him of this error. We may say that all laws and rules, chemical discipline, vital discipline, or social discipline, are so many additional brakes intended to restrain this omnivorous appetite of every being. In general we are rarely conscious of them, we civilized men, subjected to their tyranny from our cradles. Our ambition is aborted, crushed even in the egg, and yet how deep must it be to break forth

---

61. [Trans. Note: Tarde develops this tripartite scheme of forms of repetition at length in *The Laws of Imitation (Les Lois de l'imitation)*.]

here and there in history through the least crack in the dykes of our habit, defying centuries of hereditary constriction, in bursts such as Caesar or Napoleon I!

To come up against one's limit, to have one's impotence confirmed: what a terrible shock for every man and, above all, what a surprise! Surely, in this universal pretention of the infinitely small to the infinitely great, and in the universal and eternal shock which results, there is some ground for pessimism. For one unique development, so many billions of abortions! Our concept of matter accurately reflects the essentially frustrating (*contrariant*) nature of the world around us. The psychologists are right, more right than they know: external reality exists for us only by its property of *resisting* us, a resistance which is moreover not only haptic, in its solidity, but also visual in its opacity, voluntative in its inobedience to our wishes, intellectual in its impenetrability to our thought. To say that matter is solid is to say that it is inobedient: despite all illusions to the contrary, it is a relation between *it and us*, and not between *it and itself*, which is described by the former attribute as much as by the latter.

Is there any hope of a remedy for this state of affairs? No, to judge by the inductions suggested by the example of our societies: inequality will rather grow more and more between the victors and the vanquished of the world. The victory of the former and the defeat of the latter will grow every day more complete. Indeed, one of the most certain indicators of the progress of a people's civilization is that the making of great reputations, great military or industrial undertakings, great reforms, and radical reorganizations become possible. In other words, the progress of civilization, in eliminating dialects and diffusing a single language, in effacing differences in customs and establishing a universal code of law, in nourishing citizens' minds uniformly by means of newspapers, which are more in demand than books, and in a thousand other ways, essentially facilitates the ever more complete, ever less fragmented realization of a unique individual plan by the whole mass of the nation. Hence, thousands of different plans which might, at a less advanced stage, have made a step towards fulfilment concurrently with the destined victor, are doomed to be fatally stifled. John Stuart Mill says very well in his *Principles of Political Economy*: 'In proportion as [human beings] put off the qualities of the savage, they become amenable to discipline; capable of adhering to plans concerted beforehand,

and about which they may not have been consulted; of subordinating their individual caprice to a preconceived determination, and performing severally the parts allotted to them in a combined undertaking'.[62]

At length, after many centuries, we can see to what point nations should be conducted by such progress: to a degree of icy splendour and pure regularity which is almost mineral or crystalline, and which forms a striking contrast to the bizarre grace and the deeply alive complexity of their beginnings.

Leaving such speculations aside, and confining ourselves to positive facts, the formation of each thing by propagation starting from a point is not in doubt, and justifies us in admitting the existence of *leading elements* (*éléments-chefs*). It will be objected that it is difficult to discover, among the myriad subjects of one of these stellar or molecular, organic or urban States which I imagine, the true master, the founder, centre and focus of these spheres and radiations of similar actions, which are repeated and regulated harmoniously. This is because in reality there exist an infinite number of centres and foci, from different points of view and to varying degrees. To consider only the most important of these centres, there still exists, we maintain, at the heart of the sun, the conquering atom which by its individual action extended by degrees to the whole primordial nebula, disrupted the contented state of equilibrium which, we are told, the latter enjoyed. Little by little, its attractive influence created a mass, while around it other atoms, its crowned vassals, followed its example in separately gathering together several fragments of its vast empire, and shaped the planets. And, since this first beginning of time, have these triumphant atoms, imitated by their slaves who exert their own attractive power, ever ceased for an instant their attraction and vibration? In spreading like a contagion through infinite space, has their condensatory power diminished? No, for its imitators are not only its rivals, but its collaborators.

Likewise, what prodigious conquerors are the infinitesimal germs, which succeed in submitting to their dominion a mass millions of times greater than their minute size! What a treasury of admirable inventions, of ingenious recipes for the exploitation and direction of others, emanates from these microscopic cells, whose genius and whose smallness should equally amaze us!

---

62. [Trans. Note: J. S. Mill, *Principles of Political Economy*, IV.1, vol. II, 5th ed., London, Parker, Son & Bourn 1862, p. 261, §2.]

But when I speak of conquest and ambition with respect to cellular societies, it is rather of propaganda and devotion that I should speak. This is all metaphorical, of course, but nonetheless one should choose one's terminology and points of comparison wisely; and moreover I would ask the reader not to forget that, if belief and desire, in the pure and abstract sense in which I understand these two great forces, the only two quantities of the soul, have the universality which I ascribe to them, it is barely metaphorical to use the term *idea* for the application of *belief-force* to internal *qualitative indicators* (which, however, bear no relation to our sensations and images)—the term *intention* for the application of *desire-force* to one of these quasi-ideas—the term propaganda for the communication from element to element, not of course a verbal communication but of unknown specific character, of the *quasi-intention* formed by an originating element,—the term conversion for the internal transformation of an element into which there enters, in place of its own quasi-intention, that of another, and so on. Bearing these remarks in mind, let us proceed.

When an empire wishes to extend its power, it sends, to a single point on the globe and not a large number of points at once, not a single man but an enormous army which, once this point is conquered, directs elsewhere its force of devastation. By contrast, when the leader of a religion wishes to disseminate it, he sends out missionaries as widely as possible, to all points of the compass, to create a widely dispersed body of isolated men charged with announcing the good news and winning souls by persuasion. Now, I submit that, in this respect, the processes by which living things propagate themselves resemble apostolic propaganda much more than military annexation. And, if one adds to this point of similarity a hundred more, if one observes that each living species, like a church or a religious community, is a world closed to rival groups, and yet hospitable and avid for new recruits,—a world which is enigmatic and undecipherable from the outside, where mysterious passwords known only to the faithful are exchanged,—a conservative world in which all must conform scrupulously and indefinitely, with remarkable selflessness, to the traditional rites,—a world which is highly hierarchical, yet whose inequalities seem never to provoke rebellion—a world at once highly active and highly regulated, highly persistent and highly flexible, capable of adapting readily to changes of circumstance and yet persevering in its age-old beliefs; then it will be clear that I am not abusing the freedom of analogy by comparing biological phenomena to the religious dimensions of our societies rather than to their military, industrial, scientific or artistic aspects.

In certain respects, an army resembles an organism just as closely as does a convent. The same discipline, the same rigorous subordination, the same power of group solidarity, pertain in an organism as in a regiment. The mode of *nutrition* (that is, recruitment) is also the same, by *intussusception*, by the periodic incorporation of recruits, filling the structure to a quota which is never exceeded. However, in other no less important respects, the difference is striking: regimentation transforms and regenerates the conscript less than nutritive assimilation does the alimentary cell, or religious conversion the neophyte. Military education never penetrates the conscript's inmost heart. Hence the lesser persistence and shorter duration of military organizations. Even in barbarian societies, their transformations are somewhat abrupt and frequent, unless they are in a wholly undeveloped state, in which case their incoherence prevents us from comparing them to living things, even the simplest. Finally, when an army grows, when a regiment reproduces, this reproduction never takes place, as does that of living things, by the emission of a unique element around which foreign elements subsequently gather. A regiment can reproduce only by scissiparity; a single soldier or officer, asked hypothetically to form a body of troops in a foreign country by his own efforts, would find himself absolutely unable to form a platoon of four men with him as corporal.

In virtue of these differential characteristics, life appears to us as something respectable and sacred, as a great and generous enterprise of salvation and redemption of the elements which are chained up in the tight bonds of chemistry; and it is surely to misunderstand its nature if we consider its evolution, with Darwin, as a series of military operations where destruction is the companion and condition of victory. This great and prevalent prejudice seems to be confirmed by the distressing spectacle of living beings devouring one another; upon seeing a cat's claw attack a bird's nest, the heart is deeply moved and takes to decrying life's egotism and cruelty. Life, however, is neither egotistical nor cruel and, before casting such aspersions on it, we should ask ourselves whether it is possible to interpret its most repellent actions in a way which can reconcile this horror with the admiration which we cannot but feel for the beauty of its works. From the point of view of our hypothesis, nothing could be easier. When a living thing destroys another to eat it, the elements of the destroyer intend perhaps to offer to the elements of the destroyed the same kind of service which the faithful of a religion think they offer the sectaries of another cult in breaking their temples, their clerical institutions, their religious ties, and endeavouring to convert them to the 'true faith'. What is thus destroyed is beings' exterior, the elements endowed with faith and love, but faith and love themselves are not sacrificed. In general, it must be acknowledged, it is higher forms of life which absorb and assimilate the lower, just as the greatest and most developed religions, Christianity, Buddhism, Islam, convert the fetishists and not *vice versa*.

With this concept of life, need I add how one may conceive consciousness and death? I call consciousness, soul, mind, the transitory victory of an eternal element, which by some favourable chance rises above the obscure realm of the infinitesimal, to rule a people of brothers who are now become his subjects, subjects them for a little while to his law, handed down by his predecessors and slightly amended by him, or marked by his royal seal; and I call death the gradual or sudden dethroning, the voluntary or forced abdication of this spiritual conqueror who, like Darius after Arbela and Napoleon after Waterloo, Charles V at Yuste and Diocletian at Salona,[63] but even more completely stripped bare once more, returns to the infinitesimal where it was born and whence it came, perhaps lamented, certainly not invariable and, who knows? not unconscious.

Let us not then say *the other life* or *nothingness*, let us say *non-life*, without prejudging the question. Non-life is not necessarily non-being, any more than is non-ego; and the arguments of certain philosophers against the possibility of existence after death carry no more weight than those of idealist sceptics against the reality of the external world.—That life is preferable to non-life; again, nothing is less well established. Perhaps life is nothing but a time of trials, a drudgery of schoolboy exercises undergone by the monads who, on graduating from this hard and mystical school, find themselves purged of their former need for universal

---

63. [Trans. Note: The final defeats and abdications of great imperial rulers: Darius III of Persia was defeated by Alexander the Great at Arbela (331 BCE) and Napoleon by British and Prussian forces at Waterloo (1815); Charles V, Holy Roman Emperor, retired to the monastery of Yuste in Extremadura (1556) after his abdication, and Diocletian, Roman Emperor, to his palace near Salona in Dalmatia (in present-day Split, Croatia; 305 CE.)]

domination. I am persuaded that few among them, once fallen from the cerebral throne, have any wish to return. Restored to their original state, to absolute independence, they give up their power over the body without suffering and without hoping to return, and enjoy for all eternity the divine state into which they were plunged in the last moment of life, exemption from all evils and all desires, though not from all loves, and the certainty of possessing a concealed and everlasting good.

Thus death would be explained; thus life would be justified, by the purgation of desire ... But enough hypotheses. Will you, dear reader, forgive me this attempt at metaphysics?

AFTERWORD

AFTERWORD: TARDE'S PANSOCIAL ONTOLOGY

1. INTRODUCTION

Monadology and Sociology (hereafter *MS*) is a remarkable book which has, to date, received relatively little attention, particularly in the English-speaking world. It has remained somewhat marginal to, if not entirely absent from, the remarkable resurgence of interest in Tarde's work over the last decade or so. I believe that *MS* has a substantial and as yet largely unrealized contribution to make to contemporary debates, and hope that this translation may contribute in some way to the actualization of this possibility.

This afterword, therefore, is not primarily historical. It will attempt neither to situate *MS* in Tarde's oeuvre or in its historical time and place, nor to trace the pathways of his re-emergence from the shadowy realm of once-lauded thinkers, although much useful historical work remains to be done along these lines.[1] The uncanny combination of the familiar and the strange which strikes the contemporary reader of *MS* will here remain unexplained. Rather, the primary goal is to try to establish a niche for Tarde's theory in our current philosophical ecology, and briefly to indicate some potential applications. To this end, however, a certain degree of exegesis and constructive systematization will be required, which I hope will not detract too much from the charm of the text itself.

The perspective taken will be primarily philosophical rather than sociological, and more particularly metaphysical

---

1. A (rather jaundiced) history of Tarde's reception in 20th-century France can be found in L. Mucchielli (2000) 'Tardomania? Réflexions sur les usages contemporains de Tarde', *Revue d'Histoire des Sciences Humaines*, vol. 3, pp.161-184.

orontological,[2] in the sense of seeing *MS* as offering an encompassing theory of the make-up of reality. The immediate reason for this hermeneutic choice is purely circumstantial,[3] namely that the great majority of work on Tarde, especially that published in English, has been primarily focused on his significance for debates within the social sciences;[4] his place in the sociological canon now seems assured, while some work is still required to establish a place for his thought in a philosophical context.

The possibility of the choice, however, is perhaps revealing. As I will argue, the fact that *MS*, 'the most metaphysical of the works of the most philosophical of sociologists',[5] can be read, and offer a wealth of productive insights, from either perspective, is deeply rooted in the theory it elaborates. If monadology, in Tarde's hands, is a metaphysics premised on the idea that the bonds holding reality together are essentially social, then the sociology he invokes is one which has burst its bounds and overflowed to the point where its most natural comparators are metaphysical. My hope, then, is that Tarde's thought may help to productively corrupt the illusory purity of the philosophical standpoint, at the same time as it dismantles the constellations of sociological good sense.

2. The term 'ontology' is not strictly appropriate, since it refers to the study of being (Greek *ōn, ontos*), while Tarde argues that the principle of reality is not being but having. However, it has the advantage of being broadly familiar in both philosophy and, increasingly, social theory to refer to any theoretical characterization of the nature of reality. One alternative would be to coin a new term, 'echontology' (from *ekhōn, -ontos*, having), but its (entirely fortuitous) resonances with 'echo' and 'ecology' would be distracting, if in some ways rather appropriate.

3. For a more considered account of the relation between philosophy and sociology, see D. Toews, 'Tarde and Durkheim and the non-sociological ground of sociology', in Candea, *The Social*, cited below.

4. This said, the secondary literature on Tarde even within the social sciences is still not very extensive. Two major collections are available in English: M. Candea (ed.), *The Social after Gabriel Tarde: Debates and Assessments*, Abingdon, Routledge, 2010; and the special issue of *Economy and Society* edited by A. Barry and N. Thrift (*Economy and Society*, vol. 36, no. 4, 2007). See also D. Toews, 'The new Tarde: Sociology after the end of the social', *Theory, Culture and Society*, vol. 20, no. 5, 2003, pp. 81-98; D. Toews, 'The renaissance of *philosophie Tardienne*', *Pli: The Warwick Journal of Philosophy*, no. 8, 1999, pp. 164-173. The single most useful work on *MS* in English to date is B. Latour, 'Gabriel Tarde and the end of the social', in P. Joyce, ed., *The Social in Question: New Bearings in History and the Social Sciences*, London, Routledge, 2002, pp. 117-132.

5. É. Alliez, 'Tarde et la problème de la constitution', in G. Tarde, *Monadologie et sociologie*, Le Plessis, Institut Synthélabo, 1999, p. 9.

2. PANSOCIAL ONTOLOGY AND THE PRIORITY OF RELATION

The central and most original insight of *MS*, from which all the rest of the system flows, is that all of nature, organic and inorganic, at all scales from atoms to stars and galaxies, consists of societies. This thesis implies the slightly less original but no less challenging theory that every entity has some form of mind, self, or subjectivity (the theory of panpsychism or 'psychomorphism').[6] Tarde uses the term 'universal sociology' to describe this insight; however, it is necessary to distinguish the basic idea that all things are societies from the theoretical toolbox required to investigate these non-human societies, which will be furnished by a generalization of sociological theory in the usual sense, and more particularly of the theory set out in Tarde's sociological works. I will use the term 'pansocial ontology'[7] for the former, which will be the primary focus here, reserving universal sociology in the narrow sense for the latter. In principle, the two are independent: one might imagine a whole range of competing universal sociologies on the basis of the same basic insight, and indeed, it can be argued that on certain points Tarde's own sociological views are in tension with the metaphysical imperatives of the system. That said, there is a continuous exchange of ideas between the two domains, making the distinction to some extent artificial, but it is of value in isolating the philosophically most distinctive contributions of Tarde's thought.

MS puts forward two arguments for pansociality (and panpsychism), one analogical and one conceptual. The argument from analogy is that reality is structured like a society, and the entities which make it up behave like living things. As Tarde notes, this analogy was familiar enough at the time of writing, in the form of the theory of society as analogous to a living organism, which was most exhaustively set out in Spencer's 'The Social Organism' but also had a broad appeal for many social theorists, and which can arguably be traced back to Aristotle's *Politics*. However, Tarde

---

6. Neither *MS* nor this afterword are terminologically exact on the vocabulary of minds and selves; *MS* uses 'mind', 'spirit' and 'psyche' and their derivatives more or less interchangeably. However, the decision not to adopt Tarde's own term 'psychomorphism' and its companion 'sociomorphism' is deliberate, since their tentativeness is belied by the theory itself.

7. The term 'pansocial' is coined (avoiding the misleading connotations of 'pan-socialist') on the model of 'panpsychist' and 'pantheist'. Not only the model: as noted, Tarde's theory is also a panpsychism, and in his own terms a 'myriatheism' (p. 25), which might be less elegantly paraphrased as polypantheism.

is not directly concerned to build on such theories.[8] Their main failing is to deploy the analogy in a limited and inverted form relative to *MS*: limited, in that the analogy is restricted to living things and not extended to inorganic nature, and inverted, in that it compares society to an organism rather than *vice versa*, in the service of an organicist theory of society rather than a pansocial theory of the organism. Thus, while Tarde avails himself of the work of these theories where they are useful, his own use of the analogy has a rather different goal. In particular, as I will argue, the point for Tarde is not to hypostasize the social or exalt its importance as against that of the individual, but to utilize the relationship between individual and society as a model for metaphysical theory more broadly.

The implications of the analogical argument for pansociality are pursued in detail throughout *MS*, and need be only briefly rehearsed here. Any physical structure perpetuates itself by similar means to a social order: through educational and institutional discipline, the manipulation of incentives, the promulgation of ideologies and the threat of violence. One might say that for Tarde, all of reality, to the extent that it endures, has the character of the Sartrean practico-inert, the cooled sediments of once fluid social interactions. This implies that the apparent stability of macroscopic material phenomena is, first, only provisional—albeit on timescales vastly greater than that of a human society or culture—and, second, the outcome of a co-ordination among a huge number of elements whose being is not exhausted by their belonging to a particular aggregate, and which collaborate more or less willingly. As Latour puts it, Tarde refuses the distinction between the law and what is subject to the law.[9] That is, rather than physical laws explaining the co-ordination and predictability of natural movements, the former are rather explained by the latter—or more precisely, they are nothing more than the social organization of the elements such that their intentions and beliefs are directed, by coercion or persuasion, towards a common goal. These ostensibly law-governed forms of organization are akin to political régimes, which may last for a considerable length of time, but will sooner or later fall victim to some form of evolutionary or revolutionary transformation.

---

8. Elsewhere he criticizes them strongly, although for rather different reasons than those which concern us here (see *Social Laws (Les Lois sociales)*, ch. I).

9. B. Latour, 'Gabriel Tarde and the end of the social'.

The panpsychist side of the analogy is set out in terms of the theory of belief and desire as 'psychological quantities'. Without going into the detail of the theory,[10] it enables Tarde to elaborate the mind- or self-like qualities of non-human things without ascribing to them, for example, a capacity for conscious thought or cognition. At the most basic level, desire is manifest in inorganic nature in the form of force, and belief as the constancy of material substance. Material bodies enter into conflicts, exchanges or dialogues with one another, changing their positions and movements as a result. The more complex systems of forces which act to coordinate and organize matter into physical or organic structures resemble institutions or ideologies which have the power to intimately shape the selfhood of their members or adherents.

As noted, however, the argument from analogy is not intended to stand alone, although it forms the basis of many of the most interesting theoretical elaborations of MS (and is not always expounded with absolute seriousness). There is also a conceptual or perhaps epistemological argument.[11] Tarde argues that we know ourselves immediately and from within not only as thinking subjects, or pointlike centres of cognition. Rather, our introspective self-knowledge is already complex and structured, in two ways. First, we are both mind and body, embodied minds or animate bodies. Second, we are members of a society, participants in a culture, and speakers of a language. He concludes by arguing that this immediate knowledge of ourselves is the only reliable knowledge of being we have, and in fact that the only way we can understand what beings are is on the analogy of our

---

10. Further detail can be found in Tarde's essay 'Belief and Desire ('La Croyance et le désir', in *Essais et mélanges sociologiques*). On my reading, the value of this theory of 'psychological quantities' is heuristic rather than foundational; I would also argue that, considered as an ontological postulate rather than a methodological guideline, it is one of the weaker points of the argument. However, other readings place much greater emphasis on this aspect, including those as different from each other as Lazzarato's and Latour's (M. Lazzarato, 'Gabriel Tarde: un vitalisme politique', in G. Tarde, *Monadologie et Sociologie*, ed. cited; B. Latour, 'Tarde's idea of quantification', in Candea, *The Social*, cited above).

11. In a fuller exposition, this argument might be reconstructed in a number of forms, for example, as a transcendental argument or one from conceptual parsimony. Hartshorne, following Whitehead (and independently of Tarde), nicely summarizes the general idea: 'If feeling is the most general category of the immediately given, then we can form no more general category by which to describe existence in general than this very character' (C. Hartshorne, *Whitehead's Philosophy*, Lincoln, University of Nebraska Press, 1972, p.28).

own being, which is defined primarily by the relations of body to mind and of individual to society.

The implications of this argument can be seen at both logical and ontological levels. The logical implication is that relation is prior to being (this, again, is why 'ontology' is not a strictly accurate term for the Tardean theory). The idea of an entity which exists in itself is logically posterior to the complex structures of the ensouled body and the social person, although simpler to describe. In particular, the ideas of mind or material object, or person or society, do not pre-exist this relation but rather are constituted by and within it. The ontological implication is that the basic nature of reality is animate and socially connected. For certain purposes one may wish to abstract from this fundamental truth—for example, in positing purely material things with no psychic aspect—but this will be at the cost of ignoring their basic, relational, reality.

As against a large part of the mainstream philosophical tradition,[12] then, we do not first encounter ourselves, then a material reality outside ourselves, and then other persons or selves as the exterior of that exterior, but rather encounter first ourselves as social and embodied beings, and then material reality as an abstraction from this social embodiment. It is at this point that the conceptual argument for pansociality rejoins the argument from analogy. Tarde sees the supposed characteristics of the physical world—the forces of gravity or magnetism, or the solidity of matter itself—as humans' introspective self-perceptions, externalized and congealed to the point where their true origin is obscured. As much as an animistic re-enchantment of the cosmos, this might be seen as an extension of the Xenophanean or Feuerbachian critique of religion to the domain of physics. Where generations of social scientists have followed Vico in holding that society is more intimately and hence more adequately known than the natural world, if less precisely, Tarde radicalizes this argument to the point where only society is known, and the natural world can be known only insofar as it is itself composed of societies.

Tarde elucidates the specificity of his position here (pp. 16ff.) by comparison with the panpsychist but non-pansocial monistic ontologies popular in his own time, which generally rest on some form of dual-aspect strategy: that is, they hold that there is a single (type of) substance, which has thought and materiality or

---

12. Roughly, the part which goes from Descartes to Husserl; see the latter's sixth *Cartesian Meditation*.

extension as attributes, aspects, or descriptions, and thus that all material things are capable of thought.[13] The problem with such theories is that the concept of thought has no ontologically significant meaning in its own right, but derives its content purely from an introspective sense of selfhood: hence it tends to become a pure interiority without empirical content, merely doubling what is already known with an illusion of depth. Indeed, for some of its 19th-century proponents this lack of content seems to have been a major point in its favour, in that it facilitates the reconciliation of Christian or quasi-Christian doctrines of an immaterial and immortal soul with an avowedly materialistic account of the nature of reality.

By contrast, the social-individual and mind-body relations are both known immediately and introspectively and have complex ontological structures of their own. Hence, our introspective knowledge of our own being is not separate from our understanding of the rest of reality, but of itself provides the logical blocks from which the latter is built. As *MS* sets out to explain, the nature and coherence of the universe as a whole can be constructed from this basic relation. These two monolithic dualisms, mind against matter and structure against agency, whose irresolution is the original sin of ontology and social theory respectively, are not resolved by the pansocial theory so much as generalized, and the tension they generate harnessed to the motor of cosmic evolution.

3. TARDE AND LEIBNIZ

Pansocial ontology builds upon the work of previous thinkers within the philosophical tradition. Space precludes an extensive attempt to situate Tarde with respect to that tradition (or to construct a monadological counter-tradition), and I will restrict myself here to his most obvious predecessor, Leibniz. While *MS* does not set out the connection at any great length, there is obviously a substantial debt, and the several continuities between the two systems are of assistance in interpreting the theory of *MS*. There are three primary points of contact: the essentially composite nature of reality; the idea that substances must be souls, with the concomitant

---

13. Such panpsychist monisms are by no means moribund, as demonstrated by the work of Galen Strawson. These ontologies are sometimes described as Spinozist; this seems wrong to me, for the reasons set out in the remainder of the paragraph.

sharp distinction between real substances and aggregates; and the idea that every substance is affected by every other.

There are clearly also some points of divergence: Leibniz' tendency to reduce external relations to internal ones—famously expressed as 'the monads have no windows' (*Monadology* §7)—seems uncongenial to Tarde, given that, as we have seen, he sees relation as the fundamental reality. (This said, Leibniz did take himself to be elucidating the ordinary concept of relation, rather than explaining it away.) Leibniz' strong emphasis on the invariability of the laws of nature, and his conviction that the age of miracles is over, is also a point of disagreement. Finally, we might observe that Leibniz is strongly committed to the principle of sufficient reason, and to the idea that the concept of each substance embodies its whole history, while Tarde's theory emphasizes the role of unpredictable collisions in explaining the nature of reality; however, as we will see, they may not be as far apart on this point as they initially seem.

The first point which Tarde takes from Leibniz, then, is that the principles of reality are plural in nature: the most basic feature of the universe is its consisting of a multiplicity of distinct substances or elements. In other words, reality is not a continuum divided into parts, but a bringing together of entities which can in principle be understood independently of the situations they thus constitute (subject, for Leibniz, to their common dependence on God). The treatment of space and time in monadological theories is an example. Leibniz, in his debate with the Newtonian Samuel Clarke, argues that space and time are not absolute nor prior to the substances which occupy them, but relative to the relations among substances. That is, it is the relations between the monads which are basic; we then apprehend these as taking spatiotemporal form, and finally abstract the concepts of space and time in general. Along similar lines, Tarde argues against Kant that space and time are not pure forms of intuition, or a kind of matrix of experience, but are rather experienced directly as 'primitive concepts or continuous and original quasi-sensations' (p. 17).[14] A corollary of the insight that reality is composite is that the individuals which compose it must be really, and not only numerically, different: they

---

14. Tarde's formulation of this theory links space and time to belief and desire, respectively, such that physical or geometric space is one type of logical or thetic space (as for Leibniz), while the direction of time derives from the goal-orientedness of desire (see *Universal Opposition (L'Opposition universelle)*, ch. VI, sec 4).

are not only plural and distinct, but heterogeneous, such that each is in principle distinguishable from all others.

The second point in common is that substances are souls, which was examined in its Tardean form in the previous section. The desire to 'spiritualize the universe' (p. 16) which both systems manifest is perhaps the most obvious point of commonality in terms of traditional ontology, but there is more tension in this aspect of the relationship than might appear at first sight. For one thing, Tarde is not committed, as Leibniz is, to denying the reality of the material as such. More deeply, Leibniz' argument for this conclusion places a heavy weight on the idea of unity and its co-priority with being. That is, substance, or real entity, must be a unity: 'what is not truly *one* entity is not truly one *entity* either' (letter to Arnauld, 30 April 1687). A material thing cannot be said to be truly one, since it is divisible; only an entity with a substantial form or entelechy akin to a human soul or self can be said to be a substance. The Leibnizian ontology is therefore akin to the Tardean in resting on a sharp distinction between substances and mere aggregates, and in its insistence on tracing back the reality of the composite to the elements of which it is composed;[15] and for both thinkers, this is closely linked to the panpsychist ascription of mind-like qualities to all elementary substances. However, the path which Leibniz traces—the plurality and distinctness of the elementary substances implies their independent reality, which implies their unity and coherence, which implies their kinship with mind—is oblique to the Tardean argument, which rather rests on the basic relational complexity of the embodied mind.

Regardless of this divergence, many of the corollaries which Leibniz draws from this argument are also taken up by Tarde. Three points are particularly relevant. First, the mind- or self-like qualities of the elementary substances admit of degree. Unlike

---

15. Tarde relates this point to Leibniz' invention of the differential calculus. The question of the relation between Leibniz' metaphysics and the calculus is an issue we cannot here address, although it clearly has implications for the Tardean system. Part of the difficulty in establishing these implications is that, while Leibniz appears to have been committed to the reality of infinitesimals, the only viable interpretation of the calculus in Tarde's time was the theory of limits, which preserves the mathematical utility of the method while not requiring the analyst to work with real infinitesimal quantities (and which still stands as the foundation of standard analysis, but now co-exists with the non-standard analysis introduced by Abraham Robinson in the 1960s, which treats infinitesimal quantities as perfectly valid entities).

the Cartesian world, in which subjects endowed with mind are sharply separated from material reality (including non-human animals), the Leibnizian is composed of monads of various levels of perfection, from human souls through animal souls to the lesser monads of the inorganic world. Second, a complex being such as a living organism should be thought of as a complex arrangement of monads within which there is a single directing monad (the organism's soul) and a large number of subordinate monads which correspond to the various bodily parts, a hierarchical arrangement which is also of value in explicating Tardean monadology. Third, these mind-like qualities are not exhausted by conscious states: below the threshold of consciousness, there exist percepts (for Leibniz) or beliefs and desires (for Tarde) which are different only in degree from those which actually form part of experience.

The final point is that, for Leibniz, every monad is related to every other and contains a representation of any other, such that they mutually reflect each other to the greatest possible extent, and each one contains the whole universe *in nuce*. However, in line with the preceding point, some relations are much closer, and some representations much clearer and more adequate, than others. To borrow a formula from an earlier monadologist: 'everything is in everything, but appropriately' (Proclus, *Elements of Theology* §53). Tarde makes his commitment to this general principle clear in *MS* ch. III, and as I will argue, it plays a key role in the structure of his system, albeit in a very different form.

4. ELEMENT AND AGGREGATE

The comparison with Leibniz helps to focus attention on the strong emphasis of Tarde's theory on the elements of reality. What are these elements? At first sight, Tarde (like Leibniz) may seem to offer contradictory answers. For example, he sees individual human beings as both exemplary monadic elements—this is indeed one of the bases of the theory, as already noted—and as composed of numerous elements. The key to resolving these difficulties is to recall the priority of relation. It is not the element itself which is the basis in Tarde's theory but its relation to the social aggregates of which it forms a part. Thus, the emphasis on identifying the elementary components of reality does not require singling out a class of entities which are elements in an absolute sense, although this will generally be possible and useful once the domain of the relation is held fixed, and there need be no contradiction in a single (type of) entity standing in this relation in both directions, being an element while also being composed of elements.

Thus, when Tarde says that the principles of reality are to be found in the domain of the 'infinitesimal', he means this term to be taken literally, in that the elements are smaller than any assignable quantity or entity which can be identified, but also as relative to a particular perspective.[16] In this sense, the elements are whatever exists on the scale smaller than the one which is the current focus of one's attention. '[T]hese ultimate elements which form the final stage of every science ... are ultimate only from the point of view of their particular science' (p. 8). So, for example, if one's interest is in human societies or animal species, the element will be the individual human or animal; if in an organism, the cell; if in material entities, the atom; if in spatiotemporal reality in general, it will be the infinitesimal in the usual sense of the term. The fact that the notion of element does not pick out a privileged stratum of reality independently of a specific perspective is reflected in Tarde's conviction that scientific explanation cannot, in principle, ever find an ultimate reality at which it can rest. The discovery of ever-smaller organisms, he hints, may not come to an end with single-celled animalcules. Similarly, the discovery or theorization of ever more basic building-blocks of matter will not end with the atom, which will itself, sooner or later, be found to have a composite structure.[17]

Tarde's ontology of the elementary can thus be seen as a middle way between holistic doctrines of emergent properties, which grant the aggregate properties not present in the elements, and reductionisms which identify a class of entities as basic and attempt

---

16. We could go one step further here and see the elements as *purely* differential or functional (this reading is suggested by Deleuze, *Difference and Repetition*, trans. P. Patton, London, Athlone, 1994, pp. 313-314, and developed in more detail by D. Debaise, 'Une métaphysique des possessions: Puissances et sociétés chez Gabriel Tarde', *Revue de Métaphysique et de Morale*, vol. 60, no. 4, 2008, pp. 447-460, and I. Joseph, 'Gabriel Tarde: Le monde comme féerie', *Critique*, vol. 40, nos. 445/446, 1984, pp. 548-565). However, this reading seems to me to abstract too rapidly away from the role they play in specific contexts, and hence to lose much of what is distinctive in the ontology of *MS*, particularly regarding the monads' tendency to universalization (see below).

17. Of course, while the biological point has fared less well, the physical point is convincingly borne out by subsequent history. Even today, it is not implausible that the most basic particles currently known, quarks and leptons, may have some composite substructure (models positing such structure have been widely canvassed and explored empirically at the Large Hadron Collider and other sites, although at currently attained energy levels, little confirmation has been forthcoming).

to construct others from them.[18] He argues strongly and explicitly (against holism) that the element is ontologically prior to the aggregate, but as argued above, pansocial ontology also implies (against reductionism) that the relation between them is prior to either of its terms, as the relation between the individual and society is prior to either as an entity. This priority of the relation over the relata is reflected in the vertiginous opening-up of ever smaller scales beneath whatever stopping point we might have hoped to form the basis of our explanations.

The absence of a real final term to the series also, to some extent, undermines the attempt to domesticate it by thinking in terms of nested levels of reality, of the form atom-molecule-protoplasm-cell-organism-society (although MS does sometimes talk in such terms, particularly ch. VI) and the concomitant tendency to see pansociality itself through the prism of the hierarchy, such that lower levels are societies in progressively more simplified and attenuated ways.[19] Rather than filtering downwards in stages from the paradigmatic case of human persons and societies, the panpsychist and pansocial analogies radiate outwards, and illuminate each case anew. The ontological structure induced by the analogy might be compared to the traces of the more perfect radial symmetry of supposedly lower forms which Nature retains beneath the bilateral symmetry evolved for locomotion (ch. IV).[20]

Thus, despite the priority of element to aggregate, there is a balance of power between the two in each domain of the Tardean universe. To discern this balance within the various scientific theories covering these domains will require some shifts of emphasis. In some cases, Tarde will need to argue against a too strong subordination of elements to structure, as with the biological thought of his time, where the prevailing emphasis on the unity and self-organizing capacity of the organism must be countered

---

18. As already noted, Durkheimian sociology is the paradigm of holism; examples of reductionism in the sociological context might be individualisms of the rational-choice type, and in philosophical ontology the various flavours of physicalism.

19. There is reason to think that these hierarchical ontologies are the perennial temptation of monadological thought. They were also more a feature of Tarde's philosophical surroundings than may appear at first glance; although generally unpalatable to 19th-century tastes in their raw Renaissance-Neoplatonist form, they retained considerable appeal when sublimated into a historical narrative, as in Cournot's *Treatise* or, come to that, Hegel.

20. This might be described as 'the lost symmetry of the blastosphere' (J. G. Ballard, *The Atrocity Exhibition*, St Albans, Triad Panther, 1979, p. 14).

with an assertion of the independent viability, in principle, of the elements which constitute it. Edmond Perrier's theories of evolution by aggregation into colonies provide a useful support at this point. Sociology is another example, and an analogous argument forms the core of Tarde's critique of Durkheim. In other cases—and particularly in the case of inorganic nature—the monadologist will be arguing for the presence and relevance of structures which are logically irreducible to the action of mechanical forces on otherwise inert bodies, and which can only be explained by appealing to the capacity of these bodies to enter into relations of association, emulation or competition.[21]

Another, more dynamic, way of seeing this relationship is in terms of difference and identity, or heterogeneity and homogeneity. Tarde argues along Leibnizian lines that numerically distinct monads must also be qualitatively different. Thus, Tarde argues, it must be possible in principle to distinguish any two distinct atoms of the same element (using 'element' here in the conventional sense), even if this cannot be achieved in practice due to the grossness of our instruments. Due to our epistemic and sensory limitations, our experience of the world of aggregates contains sizeable tracts of homogeneity, but the belief that this homogeneity can be read back into the elements arises from an anthropocentric prejudice which will dissolve in the light of a more adequate knowledge, as the indistinct murmur of the forest resolves into the combination of the voices of the individual leaves (p. 45).[22] The heterogeneity of the elements underwrites their priority over the aggregate, in the sense that if they were perfectly homogenous, their shared form as expressed in the aggregate would exhaust their being and hence have a good claim, on the grounds of conceptual economy if nothing else, to be considered more basic than the elements.

---

21. That is, on my reading, the apparent 'reductionism' or 'individualism' of Tarde's theory is tactical rather than fundamental (although it may appear fundamental in sociological contexts—in the conventional sense of the term—and particularly in the debate with Durkheim). This seems to me a clear differend between sociologically inclined readings such as Latour's ('Gabriel Tarde and the end of the social', cited above) and more philosophical readings such as mine and Alliez', which complicate the picture of Tarde as an individualist (É. Alliez, 'Tarde et le problème', cited above; É. Alliez, 'The difference and repetition of Gabriel Tarde', *Distinktion: Scandinavian Journal of Social Theory*, vol. 5, no. 2, 2004, pp. 49-54). However, Toews sees it as a choice between (meta-)philosophical standpoints (Toews, 'The renaissance', cited above).

22. A very similar metaphor of the sound of the sea and the waves is a favourite of Leibniz' (e.g. *Discourse on Metaphysics* §33; letter to Arnauld, 9 October 1687).

This heterogeneity is not a mere logical structure, however, but manifests itself determinately in the form of an alternation with homogeneity. That is, Tarde does not simply identify the element with the heterogeneous and the aggregate with the homogenous. On the contrary, the aggregation of elements does not reliably generate homogeneity, and to the extent that it does, this often largely serves to increase heterogeneity again. Thus, heterogeneity and homogeneity, or difference and identity, mutually produce each other in a continually renewed reflection of the fundamental element-aggregate polarity. This mutual implication is not the last word, however. Tarde argues that in any given context, difference will be found to be the first and last term of the series, and in this sense is more fundamental than identity; outside of any such context, no first or last term is to be found, and thus—since identity can more readily be constructed from the aggregation of difference than difference can as the fragmentation of identity, since this fragmentation would be inexplicable except on the basis of the prior difference—the very endlessness of the alternation tends to affirm the priority of difference. (To put this argument another way: because elements can enter into relation, they are distinct; because they are distinct, as Leibniz argues, they are different; because they are different they cannot be perfectly simple, and must therefore have substructure and elements of their own, which will in turn exhibit their own differences.)

Tarde offers two analogies from human societies for the mutually productive relation between difference and identity. One is the progressive standardization of language and culture across a national territory, at the expense of local dialects and ways of life, which serves, by increasing the possibilities for interaction between individuals, to greatly expand their sphere of action and accentuate their individuality. The other is the growth of large authoritarian institutions such as armies, where the homogenization of individuals through coercive power serves to greatly amplify the decisions made by the few individuals who are empowered by the system to give orders. The two images appear contradictory in their implications; when pushed, it seems that Tarde is more committed to the first. His prediction of the terminus of this movement of homogenization in the 'crystalline' perfection of a purely transparent society (p. 62)[23] is intended to evoke not a

---

23. Tarde here (p. 29) builds on Cournot's insight that social progress tends to make society ever more predictable and law-governed, like the world of

dystopia of totalitarian surveillance, but on the contrary a vision of emancipation in which the claims of society on the individual dwindle to nothingness, and free association replaces the obligations of social life. Nonetheless, both make the same underlying theoretical point, which is that identity is ultimately for the sake of difference.

Tarde thus seems to (and has been taken to) provide support for the kinds of declarations of which have become standard across much of philosophy and social science over the last half-century, in favour of the particular rather than the general, the local rather than the universal, diversity rather than unity, and so on. However, it is instructive to note what separates *MS* from these ritualistic invocations, and hence demonstrates its real value in understanding their philosophical consequences. First, the very speculative *élan* of Tarde's text, and his willingness to make strong empirical predictions regarding, for example, the nature of molecular bonding, constitute a powerful challenge to those affirmations of diversity which remain limited to the conceptual and social domains, and are happy to accept the homogeneity of the domains of biology or physics and the invariability of their laws (and thus hypostasize a division which can never be made watertight, since human beings are also organic and material entities). Second, Tarde avoids a simple inverted reductionism, in which identity would be a mere veil over a reality of diversity. Reality is rather the productive alternation and mutual implication of the two, an alternation within which difference is determinative only in virtue of being more persistent. The priority of heterogeneity, then, licenses neither an uncritical celebration of a supposed liberation of difference from the coercion of identity—which would be only to reinscribe this identity as the unquestionability of a moral precept—nor, in general, any final reconciliation of the two, beyond their mutual conflict and constitution.

5. PROPERTY AND AVIDITY

Tarde's system, then, poses as powerful a challenge to reductionism as to holism. Indeed, it enables us to see the two as mutually reinforcing, in that they rely on the same dynamic of unveiling, the discernment of substance beneath phenomenon or cause

---

Newtonian physics, such that the transparency of the interactions of simple bodies at the base of the ontological hierarchy resonates with the transparency of social interactions at its summit.

behind effect, only pursued in opposite directions. Tarde's theory steps outside of their apparent opposition, enabling us to see both as forms of substantialism, that is, as demands to choose a certain subset of entities as principles of all the rest.[24] I have argued that this challenge is premised on the priority of relation with respect to entity. Nonetheless, if it is the dynamic of unveiling itself, rather than any specific set of ontological commitments, which is the core of substantialist metaphysics, then effectively countering the latter will require more than simply asserting the priority of relation, since otherwise there is a risk of reproducing the substantialist narrative while simply replacing entity with relation (or force or process or whatever) at its final resolution, and claiming to overcome substantialism by means of a 'dynamism' which, Tarde suggests (p. 20), is rarely satisfying even on its own terms. What is required is a positive account of relation which is sufficiently constructive to provide a coherent alternative metaphysics, while resisting the recuperation of relation into a special kind of substance. Tarde's theory of properties provides such an account.

Three stages can be distinguished in Tarde's argument. First, he observes that social relations in the general sense of the term can be thought of in terms of 'possession' or 'having', of the relationship of proprietor to property. Such relations can be either unilateral, such as that of master to slave, or reciprocal, such as that between the parties in a commercial transaction. Second, this notion of possession can be generalized to non-human societies, such that, for example, a material particle can be said to 'possess' all the other particles on which it exerts a force. The theory of possession thus generalizes the theory of belief and desire as psychological quantities; it can be seen as giving ontological content to the logical idea of relation, while retaining the generality of the latter. The other forms of relation required for scientific or metaphysical explanation can then be reconstructed on this basis: agency or causality, for example, are merely forms of possession, and are less suited to form ultimate principles because their scope is narrower.

24. This critique is what enables us to see Tarde's theory as an ontology of 'univocity', in Deleuze's terms (*Difference and Repetition*, cited above; for this connection see Debaise, 'Une métaphysique des possessions', cited above), or as a 'flat ontology' in DeLanda's (M. DeLanda, *Intensive Science and Virtual Philosophy*, London, Continuum, 2002). On my reading, however, there are considerable differences between these thinkers' development of this idea and Tarde's; space precludes a detailed engagement with this point.

Finally, the relation of substance to attribute (or 'property' in the philosophical sense) can also be reconstructed as a form of possession. The idea here would seem to be that attributes are always more or less disguised modes of relation between elements. However, these relations are themselves simply ways of describing or identifying other elements. A primary quality such as the mass of a body can be seen in terms of the gravitational force it exerts, which is really a way of describing the other bodies within its sphere of influence. A secondary quality such as a body's colour will be seen in terms of a relation to human or animal visual systems, which is the possession of the body by the latter rather than *vice versa*, and hence reduces to the operation of such visual systems. That is, as Tarde clearly says, the properties of an element are other elements, not relations with other elements.

Thus, the central image which expresses proprietorship is that of centre and sphere, not of node and link, and the overarching vision is not of an interconnected network but of a dense froth of interpenetrating spheres, in which both the circumference and the centre are everywhere. To return to the point with which I began this section, the displacement of entities by relations as the basis of reality, if it is not to slip into the reification of relations into a special kind of entity, must be doubled by a further shift from the relation to the field on which it acts. That is, while the priority of having over being certainly entails the priority of the relation of having over the entities which possess and are possessed, the still more fundamental reality is that of what Tarde calls 'avidity', or the abstract urge to possess. From the point of view of the element, it itself is the centre which emanates the sphere by projecting radii, but ontologically it is the sphere which is given, and both the centre and the radii constructed from it.

This avidity is manifest in the elements' desire to enter into relation with their peers, to gain hegemony and influence over them and to expand their spheres of action, a desire which can never be satiated, but always strives to transcend any given situation or structure. By the same token this desire is never fulfilled or completely expressed; sooner or later it will always be met by other monads' competing desires. Indeed, Tarde argues, attempts to predominate by brute force are unlikely to succeed; rather, any element can only attain even the most limited success by tactically co-opting others' drive to hegemony. Reality as we perceive it is built up out of these transactions and conflicts between avidities.

This is reflected the omnipresence of conflict, competition and exchange;[25] nonetheless, the macroscopic world in which we usually live consists largely of stable and enduring entities in reasonably co-operative relationships, which reflect the success of certain elements in gaining control over others or inspiring their emulation, and stamping their impressions on the resulting aggregates.

This avidity, however, is not a blind drive to gain power, or to reproduce, although the sexual instinct is surely one of the clearest examples of it, but contains in miniature a plan for the reorganization of the cosmos as a whole. Against the Darwinian account of evolution—which might otherwise appear rather congruent with the picture of reality sketched in the preceding paragraph—Tarde holds that every minor change, even the most fleeting and least successful mutation, has implicit within it a complete vision of the cosmos; the tiniest motion can only be understood by extending it to infinity, and the narrowest idea by drawing its most far-reaching conclusions. The drive of each monad to extend its sphere of influence is the drive to actualization of a virtual idea of the universe. '[T]he speciality of each element, a true universal medium, is to be not only a totality, but a certain kind of virtuality, and to incarnate within itself a cosmic idea which is always called, but rarely destined, to realize itself effectively. This would be, as it were, to house Plato's ideas in Epicurus' atoms, or rather Empedocles' (p. 58). Perhaps the most striking aspect of this idea is the priority it grants to the virtual over the actual. However, it is important also to note what underwrites this priority, namely each monad's having an image of the universe and a plan for its transformation, in view of which it continually acts. Thus, Tarde refuses to abandon the idea of universal explanatory principles along the lines of the Platonic Forms, but seeks to rejuvenate them by scattering throughout the universe an infinite number of copies,[26] writing in the heart of each atom an alternative virtual history of the whole, all of which are more coherent than the history which actually transpires.

By the standards of the philosophical tradition, the theory which results is curiously hybrid. On the one hand, it can be seen

---

25. The emphasis on competition is unusual in *MS* compared to Tarde's other works, where co-operative relationships are more prominent. Indeed, even *MS* (p. 25) emphasises that relations of reciprocal possession are more productive than those of unilateral possession.

26. One might think here of the Stoic 'seminal reasons' (*logoi spermatikoi*). Cf. Lazzarato, 'Gabriel Tarde', cited above, p. 107.

as a hypertrophied rationalism, where the most contingent motions can only be explained on the basis of the complete vision of reality which each monad possesses, and which it strives to actualize.[27] On the other hand, it implies that reality as a whole is very far from being rationally ordered, since it is formed in a chaotic and unpredictable fashion by the competition, and even more by the simple collision, of the trajectories of the elements. Tarde retains teleological or final causes at the level of the element even while sharply rejecting them as explanations of the history of the universe as a whole.[28]

Thus, the order which we see taking shape at macroscopic scales as a result of the temporary dominance of leading elements is both a reflection and a betrayal of the order which pertains at the level of the element. Since, Tarde argues, this order reflects the success of a leading monad in gaining predominance within a given aggregate, it represents a reinscription or projection of that monad's state on a macroscopic scale. By the same token, however, it occludes the much greater number of subordinate monads (or, more precisely, those aspects of them which are not exhausted by their participation in the aggregate), and hence by far the greatest part of the aggregate's reality. In particular, since no social order is permanent, the longer-term evolution of the aggregate will largely be determined by these subordinates, and not by the leading element. A society presents a unified face to the outside world only to the extent to which it suppresses, or at least conceals, dissent between its members.

The process which culminates in the formation of a coherent aggregate, then, does not respond to some higher or prior principles, but to the contingency of struggle; but, again, this struggle is not between two atoms of sheer will but between competing principles, or overarching visions of the universe. One implication of this is that the structural forces at work in complex aggregates tend to reflect, if imperfectly, the universal vision of the leading (and other) elements, not just the fact of dominance. Social movements without a clear programme, Tarde observes, are doomed to failure from the beginning. More than this, movements whose programme is in any way limited or particularistic are much less likely to be successful in the long term than those committed to

---

27. Lazzarato here talks of 'the priority of the logical or intellectual element over the element of will' (Lazzarato, 'Gabriel Tarde', cited above, p. 140).

28. See also *Social Laws*, ch. III.

a universal vision. Because the monads' desires and beliefs are universal in their scope, the furthest-reaching of aggregative social forces are those which have the greatest capacity to harness this universality rather than suppressing it. Whether it be the bureaucratic forms of politics which were destined to overcome charismatic monarchy, the universalism of the great missionary religions, or (to add a further example to Tarde's) the various political myths which have taken the latter's place in the 20th and 21st centuries, the most lasting and productive modes of social aggregation are those which appeal explicitly to universal visions of one form or another. Nonetheless, these visions are always severely compromised and diluted in their application; even the most harmonious is only a pale reflection of the intense drive of the individual element towards totality.

Thus the metaphysics of possession rejoins that other central tenet of monadology, that the part reflects the whole: for Tarde, it does so in the form of an urge to remake the whole in its own image by gaining hegemony over it. The reality of the particular lies in the drive towards universality, and the heterogeneity of the elements in the clash of their universalisms. The light scattered by the pulverized dust of reality resolves into an image of totality. 'What do we place within the ultimate discontinuity if not continuity? We place therein ... the totality of other beings. At the basis of each thing are all real or possible things' (p. 27).

6. THE ONTOLOGY OF ONTOLOGIES

At this point, however, there appears to be a potentially serious methodological impasse. As I have argued, the individual monads' universal visions in their pure state are only imperfectly reflected by the forms taken at an aggregate level, where the elements must either be subsumed, or fundamentally remake themselves, in the process of shaping the forms. Hence, the types of explanation which are possible at the two levels will be very different. Our understanding of the individual element will flow naturally from the unique vision towards which it tends, but, precisely because of this, will be almost entirely inapplicable to reality, since the latter is composite in nature. Conversely, our understanding of the aggregate, while pragmatically more useful, will inevitably be highly imprecise.[29]

29. We might relate this point to the Leibnizian problematic summarized by Deleuze in the form of a critique of the Cartesian principle of the 'clear *and*

If so, this implies that explanations which are fully coherent are likely to be truthful only in highly unusual cases, such as the extreme rarefaction of Crookes' 'radiant matter' state (p. 44), and conversely, that explanations which are adequate to the facts are unlikely to be coherent. Theories of highly general application (e.g. Newton's laws of motion, or the laws of natural selection) will always *ipso facto* be highly selective and partial, and, Tarde argues, doomed to failure in the very long run. To be sure, at an intermediate level, it is possible to gain some knowledge of macroscopic phenomena, but only because these phenomena are generally dominated by a leading element. However, such knowledge is partial and provisional, comparable to the knowledge we can gain of a society from official statistics; because it is dependent upon a particular ontic régime, it will be valid only until the latter's demise. Tarde thus exactly inverts the Aristotelian picture of scientific explanation as moving from the particular to the general. Rather, he argues, adequate explanations always move from the general to the particular, from aggregates to the elements which constitute them.

Now, while this may well be methodologically productive in specific contexts, it seems to rule out *a priori* any theory or explanation which claims even minimal generality. Any such theory, as outlined above, will be inevitably inadequate because it cannot escape its complicity with the movement by which the leading elements occlude the subordinate ones whence their power derives, and hence fails to see past the particular configuration to the critical potencies which germinate within it. Moreover, ontological theories, which claim to be universal explanations, would present the most egregious examples. In particular, it is hard to deny that Tarde's own theory makes highly general claims about the nature of reality, and should itself be ruled out by its own epistemological stringency, hence becoming caught in a performative contradiction.

The solution to this issue presented in Tarde's other texts[30] is

---

distinct': 'a clear idea is in itself confused; it is confused *in so far as it is clear*' (*Difference and Repetition*, p. 213, original emphasis). *MS*, however, goes further: the conflation of the distinct-obscure (the elements) which gives rise to the clear-confused (the aggregate) arises not only from an epistemic lack, but ontologically, from the interrelations of the elements themselves—which arguably also calls into question Deleuze's own, fundamentally structuralist, solution.

30. See *Social Laws*, ch. I; *The Laws of Imitation (Les Lois de l'imitation)*, ch. I. In general, it should be noted that the sharp ontological contrast in *MS* between

that the heterogeneity of the elements is compatible with the existence of large-scale repetition, and that it is these repetitions that form the basis for scientific generalization. These repetitions do not simply reflect the structures of the aggregate, but are rather present already at the elementary level. Nonetheless, within the reading developed here, this response is ultimately unsatisfying. The repetitions of the elements would seem either to be only a temporary alignment of avidities, such that the epistemological issue remains unaddressed, or to be premised on a substrate of structures or behaviors which would then be the true basis of the elements, albeit a basis of the nature of a quantity or an event rather than an entity.

A rather different resolution is suggested, if not explicitly set forth, by MS itself. The key would lie, again, in returning to the universalizing tendency of the monads. The enterprise of explanation could then be seen as akin less to the process of aggregate formation as empirically observed, than to the universal visions present within each element. In that case, the scientific or metaphysical theories we develop to explain reality would not be foreign to the elements, but on the contrary, would be profoundly continuous with the cosmic plans which form their own most intimate reality. Each element has, and in some sense is, an ontological theory of its own. Thus, Tardean metaphysics could be described as an ontology of ontologies: the universe is woven from the theorizing activity of its innumerable elements.[31] What nonetheless remains inescapable in the epistemological paradox, and must be negotiated at each stage, is that the universal drive to

---

element and aggregate is greatly softened in Tarde's other works, which are accordingly much more sanguine regarding the intelligibility of aggregative processes (e.g. imitation). Some readings would attempt to reconcile the texts by seeing the self-actualisation of the monads as simply of a piece with the formation of aggregates (thus E. V. Vargas, 'Tarde on drugs, or measures against suicide', in Candea, *The Social after Gabriel Tarde*, cited above), but this seems to go against the grain of MS. As Toews hints, MS may in this respect be ultimately irreconcilable with Tarde's sociological works (D. Toews, 'The renaissance', cited above).

31. This insight is more likely to be familiar to the contemporary reader in the context of the social sciences, where one might think of ethnomethodology's accounts of meaning-making practices, or of Viveiros de Castro's insight that 'doing anthropology means comparing anthropologies' (E. Viveiros de Castro, 'Perspectival Anthropology and the Method of Controlled Equivocation', *Tipití: Journal of the Society for the Anthropology of Lowland South America*, vol. 2, no. 1, 2004, pp. 3-22). The possibility of an ontological redeployment of such ideas is, I think, one of the most interesting directions signposted by MS.

dominate both blinds such theories to the truth of the dominated reality, and at the same time reflects the more basic truth that that reality is itself fundamentally determined by its own drive to domination, which is also a vision of how the universe ought to be. To return from the general to the particular is the goal of knowledge only because it brings more clearly into focus the particular's own knowledge of the general, and not, as the reductionist would argue, because it unveils the mute, brute truth behind the general and beyond knowledge. Our understanding of reality is ultimately reality's understanding of itself.

Finally, the ontological activity of the elements, and the combination of fundamental kinship and mutual misdirection which joins the theorist with the universe theorized, are also key to reconciling the two central theses of the priority of the element over the aggregate, and the priority of the relation between them over both its terms. The element is prior because the universal is contained within it, in a reflection which can only be discerned confusedly in the aggregate; but the relation is prior because the impulse to the universal, in which the whole being of the element ultimately consists, must pass through the aggregate (and indeed is doomed never to transcend the aggregate, be it on an astronomical scale). In this sense, the forgetfulness of theory only responds to the forgetfulness of reality, and first and foremost, that of the reality of the theorist herself. The essential occlusion and obscurity which infect any knowable macroscopic order are the obverse of the knower's own desire to possess the known, a desire of such strength that it always outweighs and eclipses the counter-desires which ultimately make it possible.

7. HUMANISM AND REALISM

In lieu of a conclusion, I would like to offer a few brief suggestions as to how the Tardean theory might usefully inform contemporary debates. I have particularly in mind the themes of humanism, or anthropocentrism, and realism. In fact I take these as essentially a single problematic, in so far as realism is defined as holding that reality is independent from human cognition or experience.[32] This is one area where Tarde's theory seems to find considerable contemporary resonance, since it has become clear that the critical project of decentring humanism, whether or not one agrees with

---

32. This definition is not entirely uncontroversial, but it saves a certain amount of time.

its ultimate goals, holds considerable promise as an analytical tool, and may find valuable support in the theory of pansocial ontology. One concern here, however, is that, as critics of post-humanism have been quick to argue, the erasure of the boundary between humans and non-humans may work less to humanize the non-human than to dehumanize the human, that is, less to extend the field of personal and moral relations from the human to the non-human than to legitimize impersonal and amoral relations to human others. Traditional organicist sociology, with its frequently authoritarian sympathies, would be a case in point. Tarde's theory does little to calm these fears, and much of it can be read in either direction. The analogy between social and natural law, for example, may be seen as an extraordinary expansion of the possibilities of social transformation beyond the wildest dreams of the utopian socialist tradition, but it could equally be taken as a counsel of despair for any struggle against injustice, which may as well seek to overthrow the law of gravity.

In any case, and aside from such abstract moralizing, the always two-sided nature of pansocial thinking means that Tarde cannot be regarded as unequivocally post- or anti-humanist. It is clear that his theory responds to the desire to situate human concerns and viewpoints within the vastly greater sweep of organic and inorganic nature, and thus to make possible a genuinely realist metaphysics. At the same time, however, it explicitly makes the human the measure of all things in the sense that inter-human social relations constitute 'the relation *par excellence*' (p. 94), the paradigm and framework for the system as a whole, for all that Tarde claims the analogical argument does not rest on specifically human facts (pp. 18ff.). Moreover, although Tarde does not posit a deep qualitative chasm between humans as cognizers and users of representational thought and a non-human reality devoid of these capacities, there is still a consequential quantitative difference. The possessive relation of the mind to the objects of its thought is in general not reciprocated, and thought enjoys a 'special dominion over the world' (p. 55). The reason for this is that possession by physical means is inevitably limited in extent; even the most massive celestial bodies can only bring so many others within their field of action. In the realm of organic life this is less true, as witnessed by the capacity of microsopic organisms to destroy physically much greater ones through infection. Cognitive representation, however, goes beyond even this in allowing the possession of any entity at all, transcending any requirement of physical presence. That is, the primacy of human societies in the theory is not merely a question of expository convenience, but reflects an inescapable fact about the place of humans in reality.

Thus, if, as argued above, the world should fundamentally be seen as a contest of theories, this contest does not take place on a level playing field; some elements and societies have considerable advantages. Moreover, this ontological fact about human beings resonates with the primary argument for accepting pansocial ontology, namely its foundation in our immediate sense of our own being—in, finally, our being human. The monadological theory, then, post-humanistically points to the contingency of its own development out of the situatedness of a text written by and for human beings. At the same time, however, as an ontology of ontologies, it elevates this contingency of theoretical elaboration to the principle of reality itself. In terms of realism, and by way of resurrecting one of its long-buried adversaries, Tarde's theory is ultimately less realist than it is social constructionist—not, of course, in that reality is socially constructed, but in that it is socially constructing, the broken surface of an ocean of sociality which far exceeds the human and yet is one with it.

www.ingramcontent.com/pod-product-compliance
Lightning Source LLC
Chambersburg PA
CBHW030053170426
43197CB00010B/1507